Dear Readers,

It is with grateful hearts that we thank all of our subscribers for your support. It is our goal to represent the many artists in the art doll industry.

We are always looking for submissions. Artists who have new works they would like to share, articles they would like to write and tutorials they would like to share are always welcome. Teaching the next generation of doll artists is very important to our industry. We would like to promote all artists who teach, so let's hear from you. Contact us:

internationaldollartists@gmail.com

Subscribe by visiting our website.

internationaldollartists.com

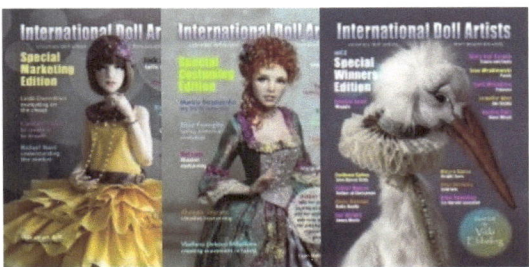

Copyright © 2017 by Cherie Fretto, Professional Doll Makers Art Guild. All rights reserved. No part of this publication may be reproduced, distributed, or transmitted in any form or by any means, including photocopying, recording, or other electronic or mechanical methods, without the prior written permission of the publisher, except in the case of brief quotations embodied in critical reviews and certain other noncommercial uses permitted by copyright law. For permission requests, write to the publisher, addressed "Attention: Publisher," at the email address below. Publisher is not responsible for unsolicited materials. Product names used are used with permission of the copyright and trademark holders, for editorial use only. No further rights are implied. All subscriptions are by download only, with printed copies on demand. Delivery will be 4 times a year as stated on our website. An email will be delivered to notify you of accessibility.

IDA Publishing ©

internationaldollartists@gmail.com
www.internationaldollartists.com

Published and printed in the USA.

Who is IDA Magazine?

Cherie Fretto: Publisher /Editor

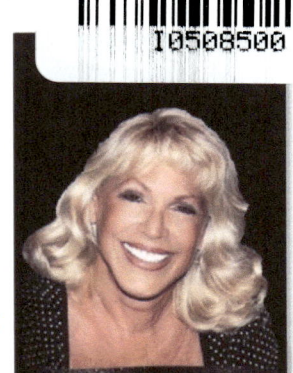

Cherie is the President and CEO of the Professional Doll Makers Art Guild. She's received many Diamond Awards for her OOAK polymer clay dolls, but specializes in BJDs, where she does her own molding and casting for limited editions.

www.BJDStudio.com

Linda Ehrenfried: Contributor

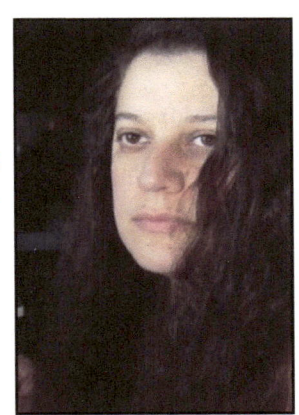

Linda is a Master Sculptor specializing in doll proportions, teaching new up and coming artists in the industry. She makes OOAK dolls in polymer clay, paper clay and mixed media.
ww.charmcityoriginals.com

Gayle Wray: Graphic Designer

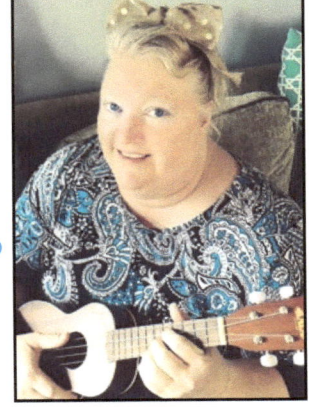

Gayle is an award-winning artist and graphic designer, author, and master cloth doll artist. She's the recipient of the Light Space & Time solo-artist showcase winner and her dolls have been featured at the Ontario Museum of History & Art.

www.gaylewray.com

International Doll Artists - May 2018—Volume 3

PDMAG Gold Awards
Winning Artists

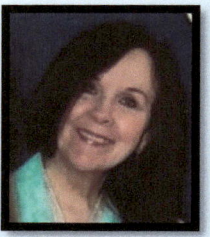
Vikki Ebbeling
Page 3

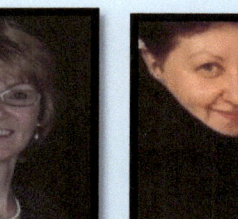
Lisa Wroblewski
Page 6

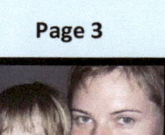
Vladlena
Page 8

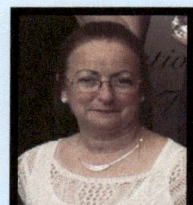
Olga Kirilova
Page 10

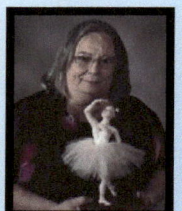
Brenda Scott
Page 13

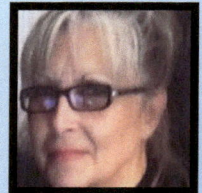
Colleen Spies
Page 17

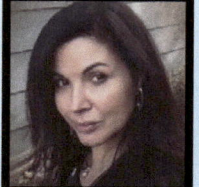
Natalie Ruiz
Page 20

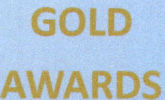
Esther Manso
Page 24

Mayra Garza
Page 28

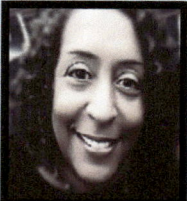
Hope Mason
Page 31

Jan Wright
Page 32

Mary Ann Banish
Page 35

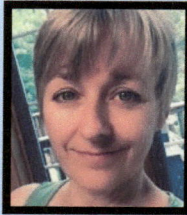
Jennifer Abel
Page 39

GOLD AWARDS

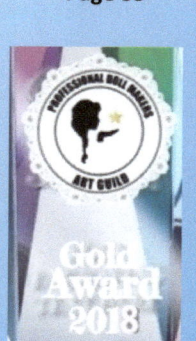

What's Inside

A look inside the Czech Republic's Panenek Museum of Dolls by Vikki Ebbeling

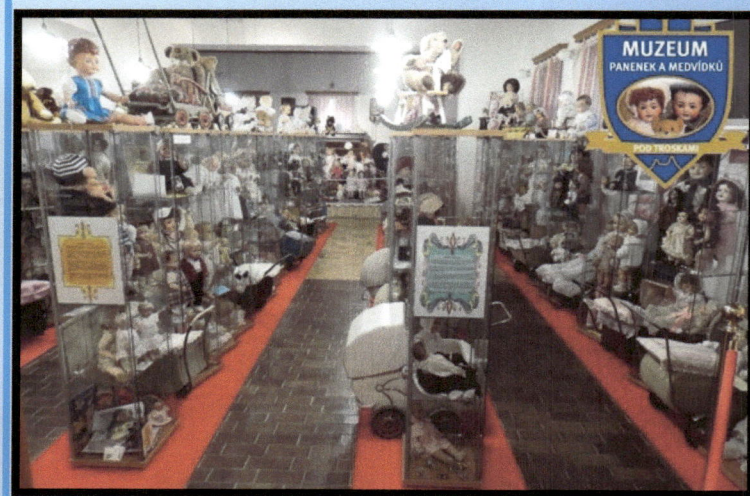

Page 50

Quarterly Quote:

The aim of art is to represent not the outward appearance of things, but their inward significance.

Artistotle

Pinnacle Awards

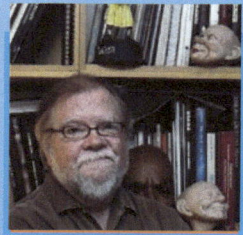
Bill Nelson
Page 46

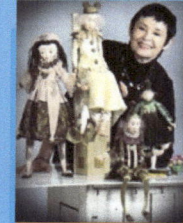
Ankie Daanen
Page 48

Vikki Ebbeling

My Adult Fantasy Fairytale:

"Sir Harold Lancelot" THE Royal Stork ...comes from a special place of Hierarchy. He delivers only "Royal babies". ...babies with the bluest of blood. Unique Rarity ... genius types of babies....with super potentials and future capabilities for ruling all lands with the most intense "Love and respect towards mankind ...and animals of all kinds. Sir "Harald Lancelot" is from the highest of nobility. But first ...he came from very humble beginnings. He was blessed by the heart of a beautiful loving Princess named "Victoria Lynn ".

One bright sunny day...She was out strolling through the royal flower gardens ...enjoying their colorful array and intoxicating fragrances. After walking for some time...She became rather warm and flushed ...so she walked on over to the shores of the lake and began to cool herself with the refreshing water. Suddenly something caught her eye.... over there ...behind the huge willow tree !!! She saw what seemed to be a very large ... egg.... which apparently looked abandoned!!! She walked towards the giant egg to investigate and noticed that it was moving and wriggling about. She became so excited ..that she could hardly contain herself!!! She knew she was about to witness a most beautiful moment-in time...the hatching of a real ... very large...baby bird !!!! How awesome was that??!!!!

She sat there wide eyed with wonder and amazement ....watching diligently as the baby emerged miraculously from its egg. It was one of the most beautiful times of her entire life.... and knowing the status of a royal princess.. that had to be pretty special. The baby bird emerged slowly.. as he gave very strong pushes with his feet and some big pecks and nudges with his beak ..until Finally he rolled completely free from his egg. Up came his wobbly head bobbing around so very helplessly. He rolled and wiggled and began to peep so loudly that the princess had to reach out to calm him. She cradled him in her hands and began to give him gentle hugs and kisses.... which comforted him into a blissful ... well earned slumber.

From that moment on he stole the heart of the princess forever. She decided to keep him and raise him for her own total pleasure. Princesses can do whatever they wish! She named him "Sir Harold Lancelot " ... for short... "Harry". He became her very own "Royal Stork". She loved him so much and spoiled him ... all she had would be his .. and she would spoil him to her hearts delight!!! Little did the princess know ....that this very SPECIAL bird....possessed some very special magical powers....... As Sir Harold Lancelot began to grow... he became magnificently beautiful. His wings became stronger and he found he could open them very wide to catch incoming air current.

One day... as he was enjoying the drifting feeling... he flapped his wings with a strong motion and began to take flight. With much excitement he flew higher and higher through the fluffy white clouds and flew straight into the heavens above. A beautiful being of light greeted him ... and announced to him of a great task he must complete. The light explained to him ...that he was to carry a miracle... a "GREAT bundle of JOY" .... to a very expectant family. He curiously peeked into the bundle and saw the most precious gift that ever could be.!!!! It was a helpless ...tiny newborn human baby. With this... the being of light ...guided him to his first baby delivery.

The Royal Stork .. now had a special purpose. And only with the greatest power of ALL ...could he bring such joy to others.

Sir Harold Lancelot .... possessed the power of "LOVE"'and spread it though out the world.

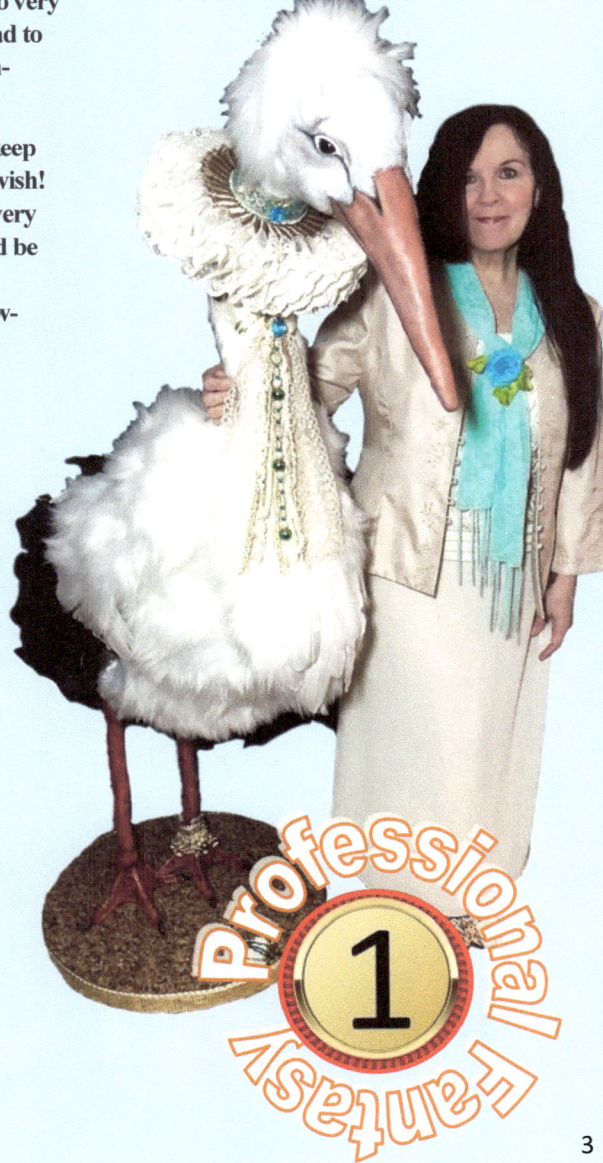

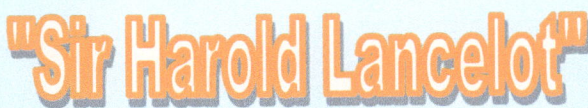

"Sir Harold Lancelot"

heavenslight4u@aol.com

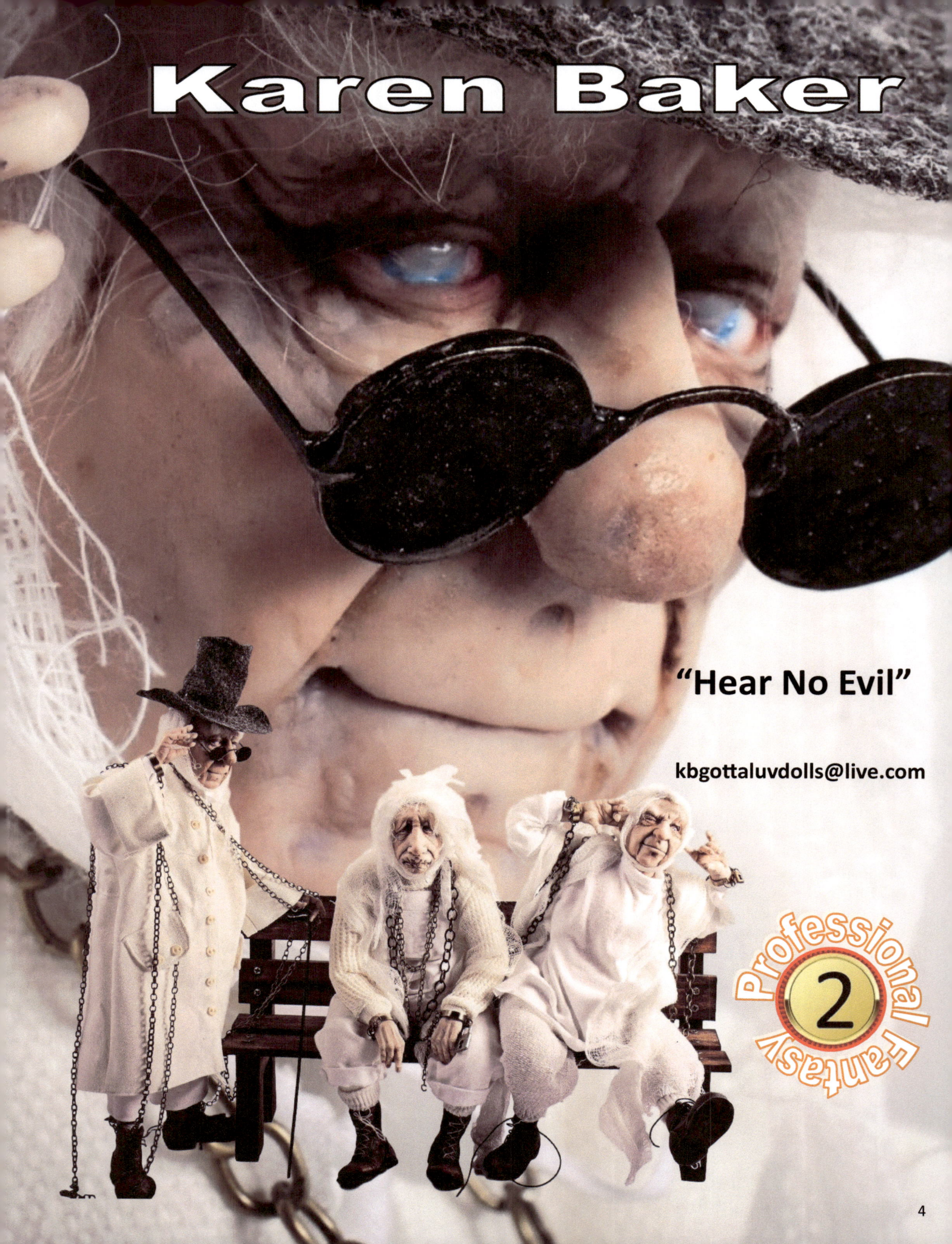

Barbara De Girolamo

"Dreaming Red Velveteen Fairy"

barbara_degirolamo@hotmail.it

Lisa Wroblewski

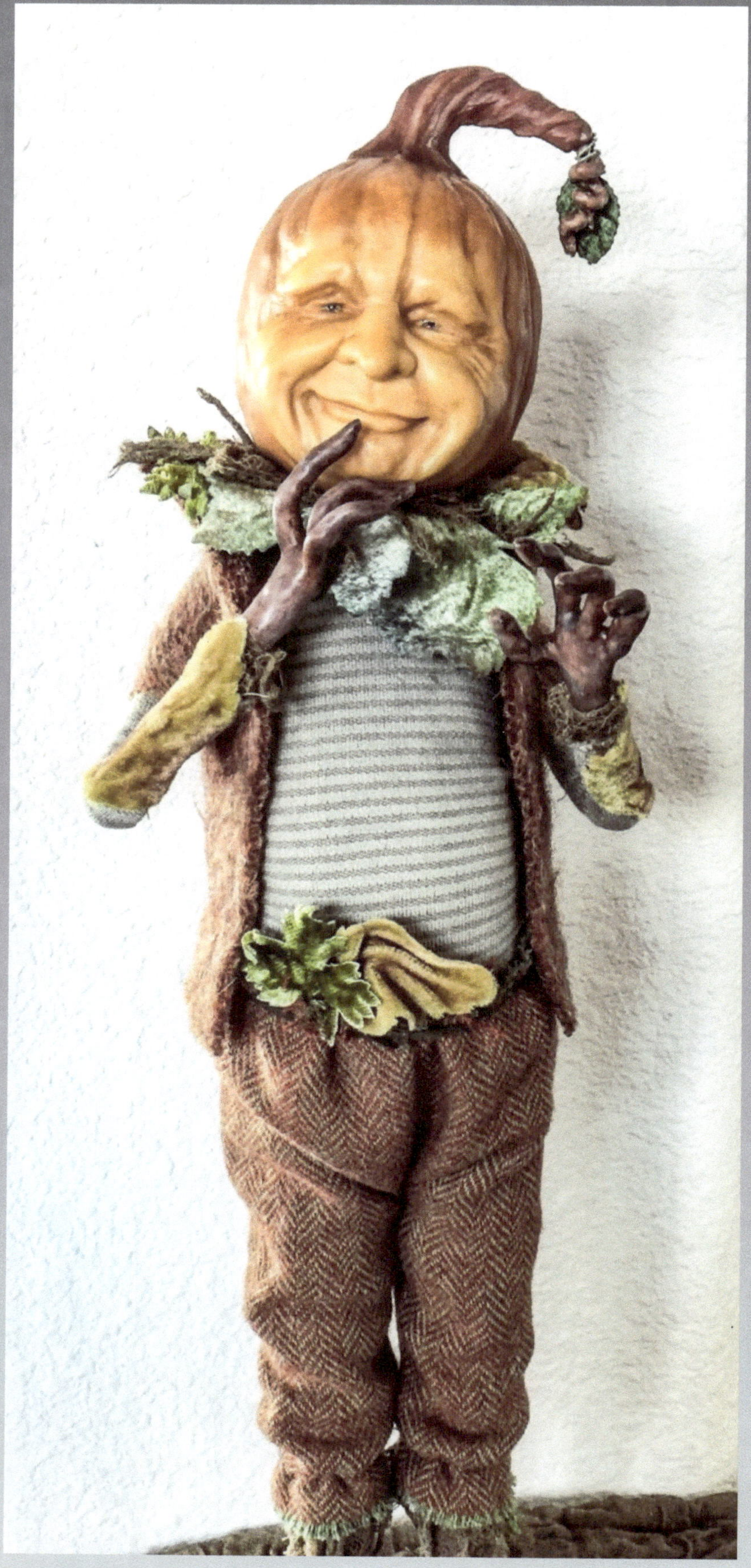

"Patch"

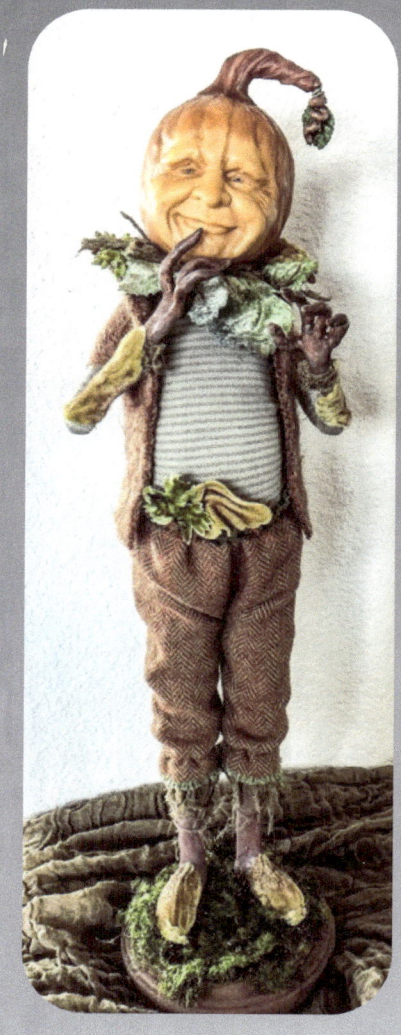

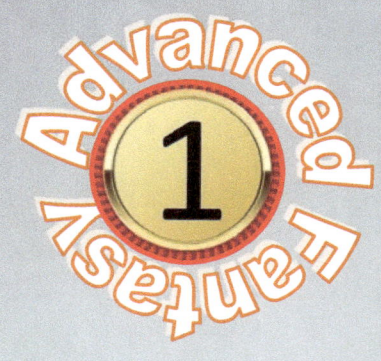

cecilandcousa@yahoo.com

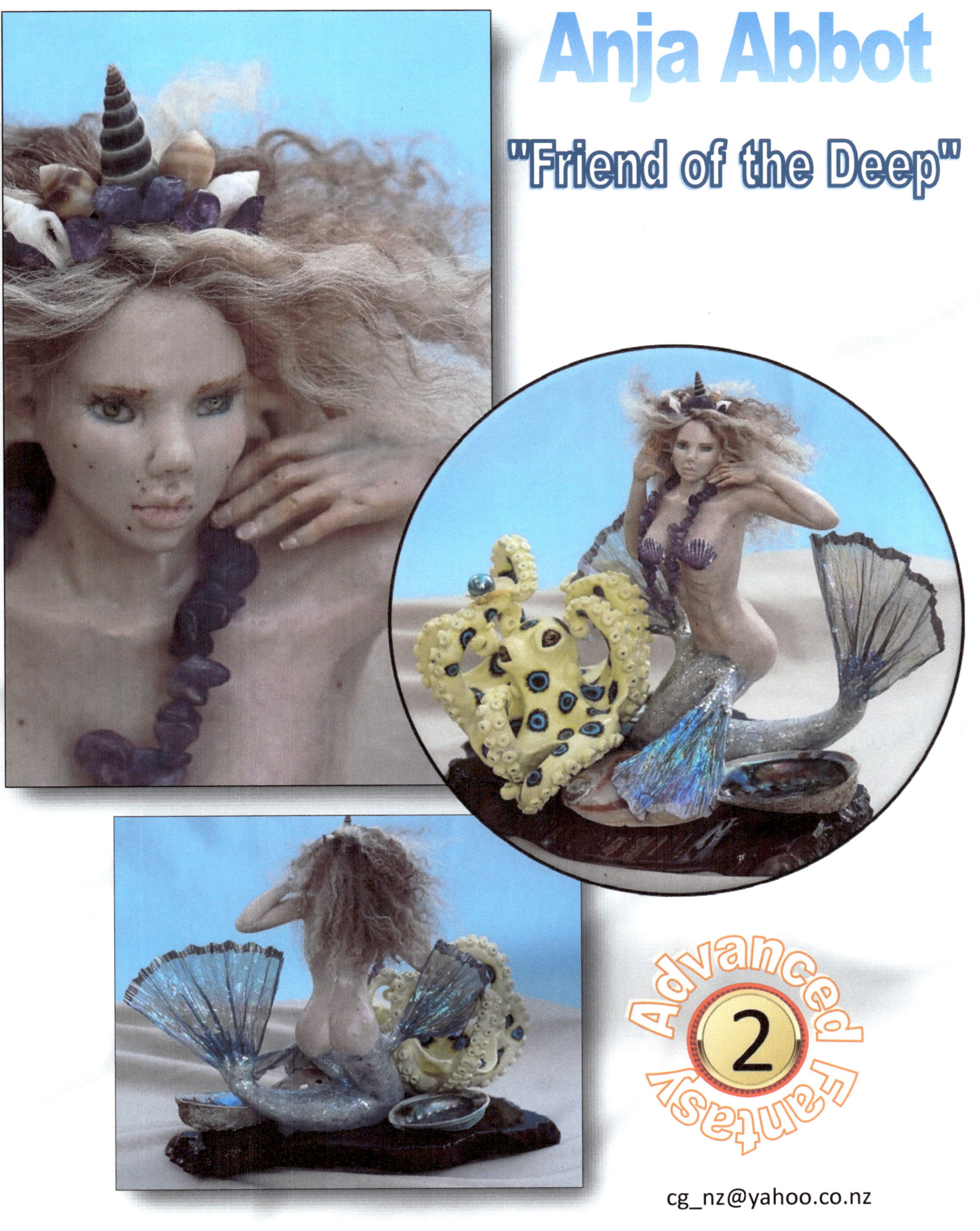

Anja Abbot

"Friend of the Deep"

Advanced Fantasy 2

cg_nz@yahoo.co.nz

"Pigasov"

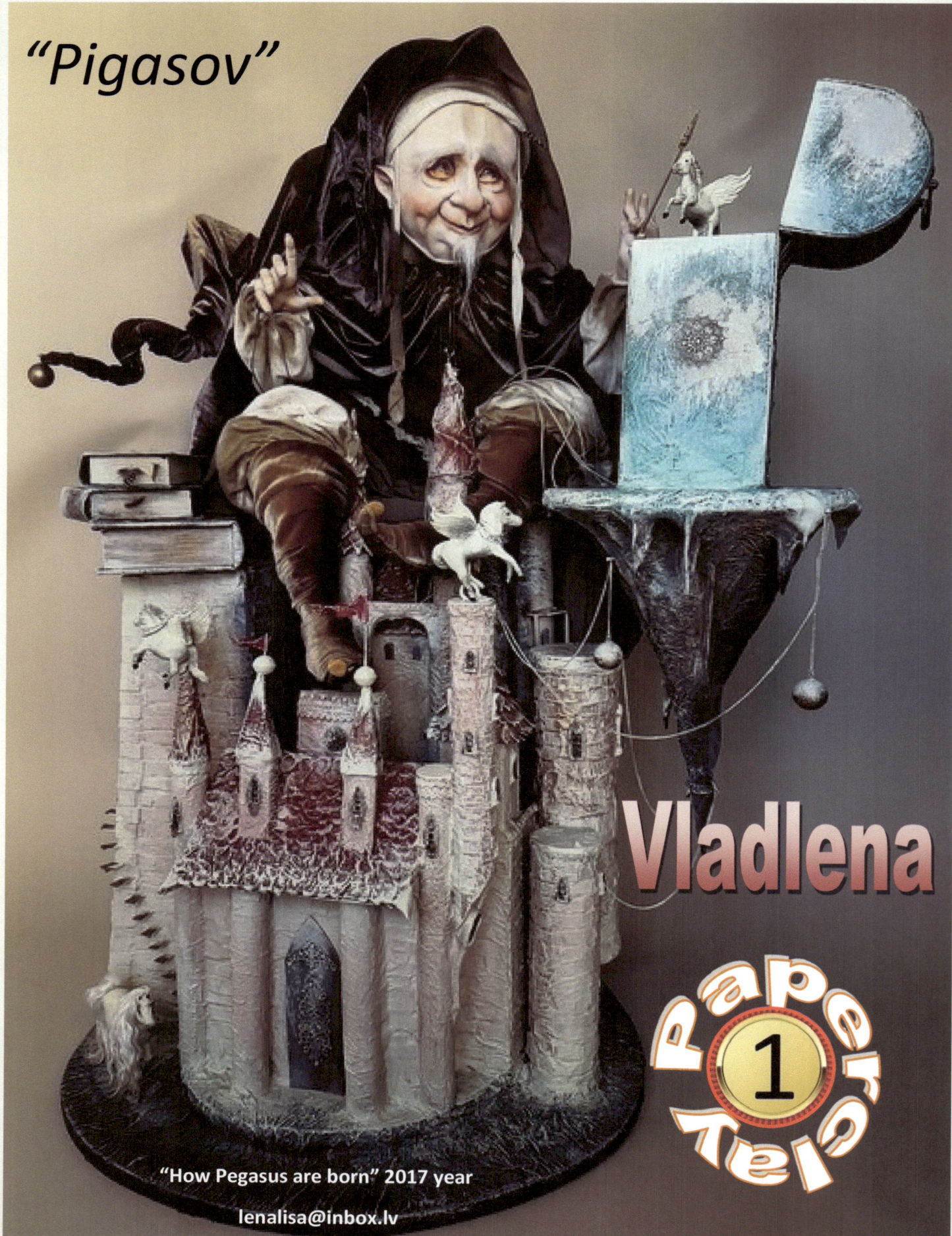

Vladlena

Papera 1

"How Pegasus are born" 2017 year
lenalisa@inbox.lv

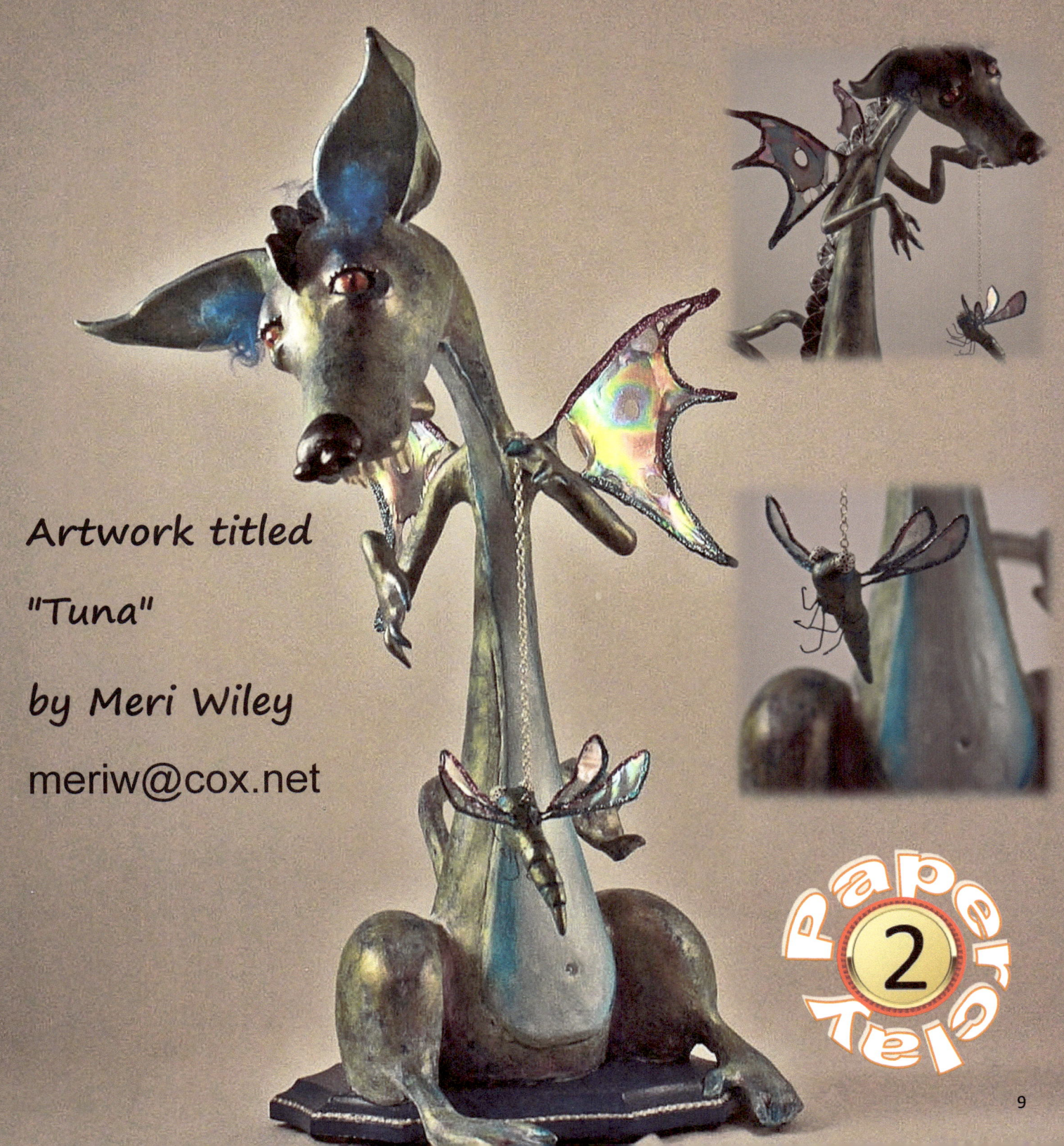

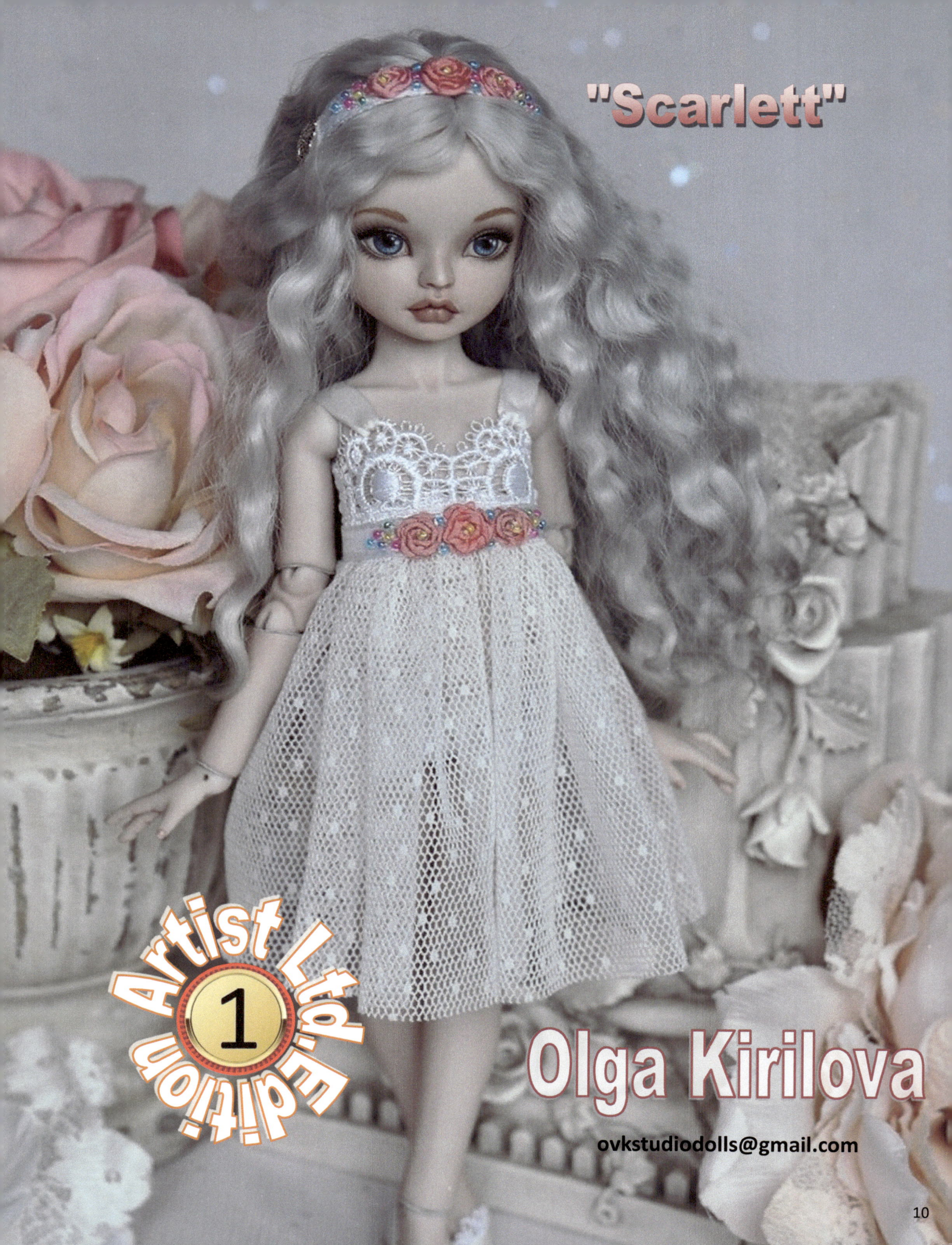

Victoria Vihareva-Pechenkina

"Silicone Baby"

I made this sculpture out of living doll polymer clay. After that, I prepared a master mold to remove the form. The mold was made with rebound which is a brush on silicone from the company smooth-on. Once cured we removed the glove mold. Unfortunately it often happens the original master is lost forever. The mold however came out perfect so there will be a limited edition of this doll made. The doll is poured via a pour hole at the top of its head in one piece. Material eco 20. Before you pour the silicone, the form needs to handle the separation of the aerosol composition. After I remove the prototype from the mold, I prepare the doll for painting. The doll is painted with silicone-based paints. The doll is painted in layers and I cure each layer in the oven. I don't leave the doll in the air, so that dust particles can form on its surface. The last layer I fix mattifying powder. The eyes are made of glass manufactured in Germany. Premium goat hair. Painted with high-quality paint. Hair is stitched on root growth. The hair is immersed in a silicone needle for routing 1-2 hair in the root of the head.

https://www.instagram.com/torydolls

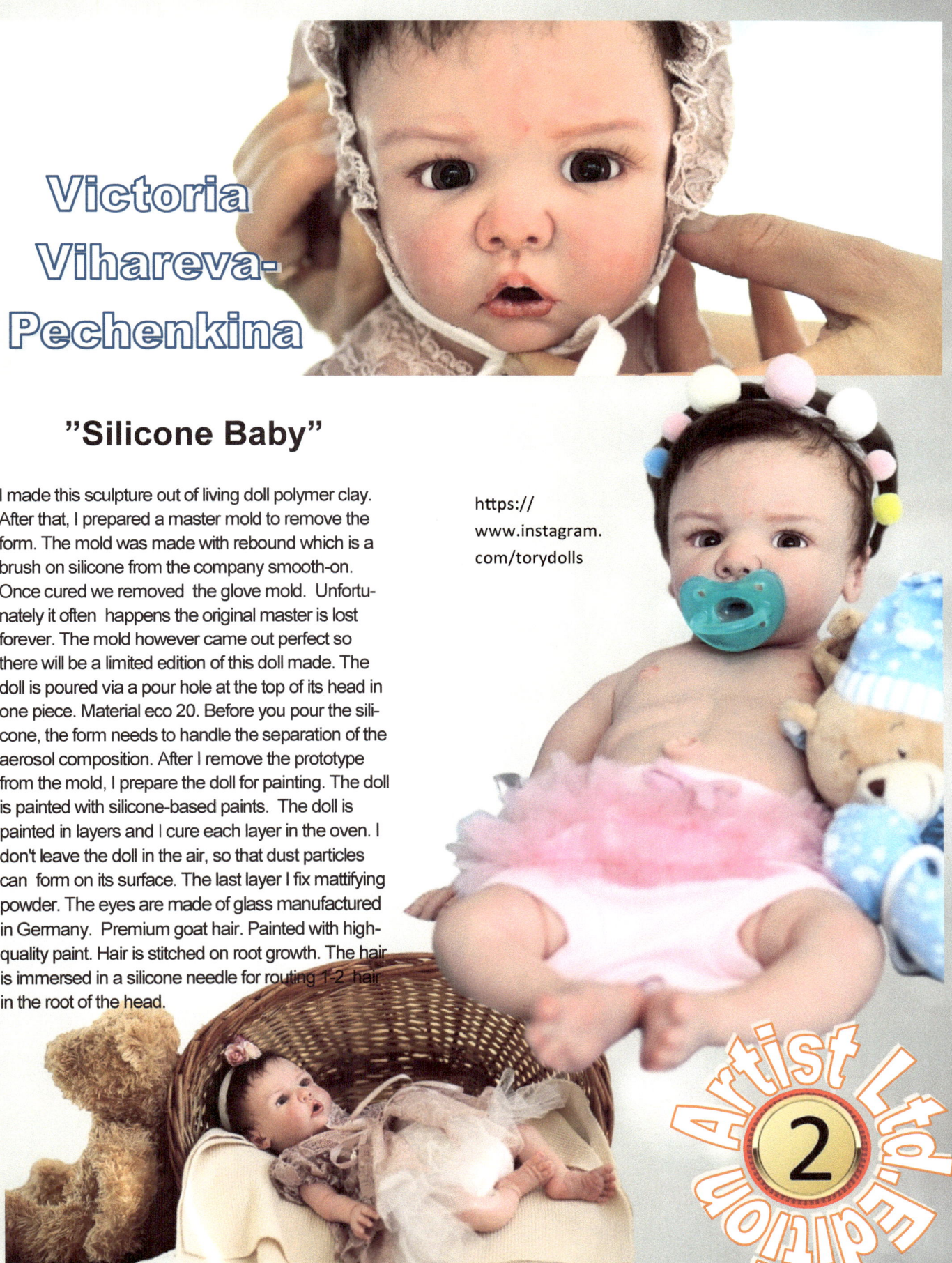

Connie Lowe

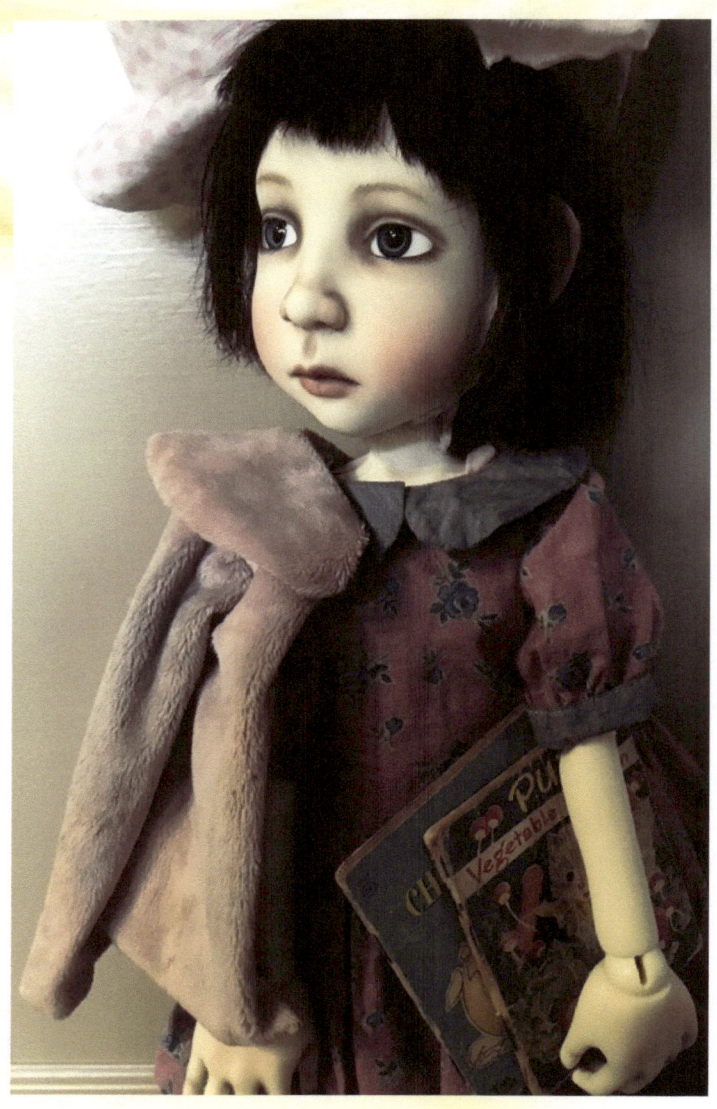

"Stella"

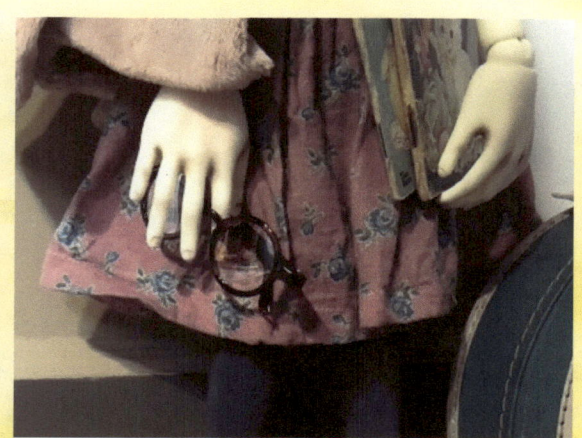

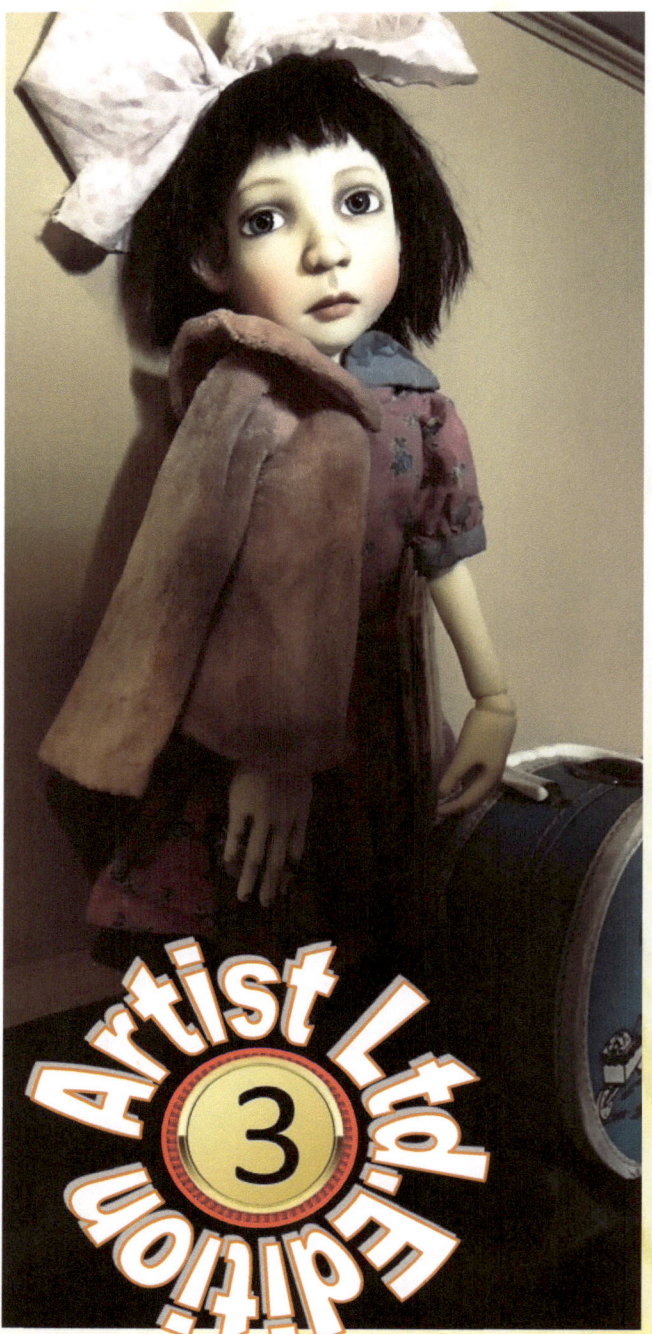

Artist Ltd. Edition 3

Paper/stone clay then resin production 20" Sculpted January 2017, released in resin May 2017 " Stella is a character BJD created to represent a depression era child. She was made in honor of my mom. Each is hand painted and dressed uniquely giving each their own personality.

www.marbledhalls.com

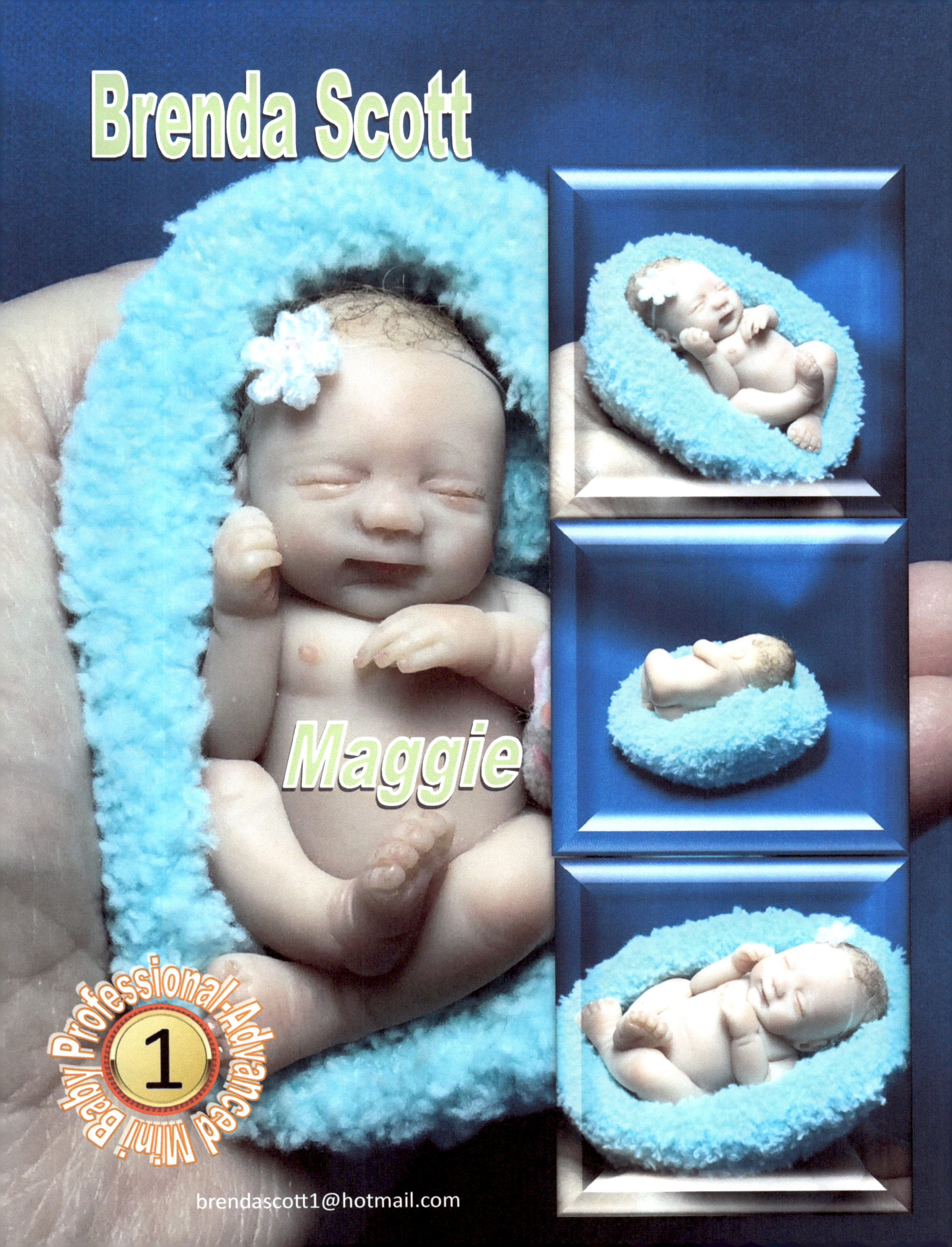

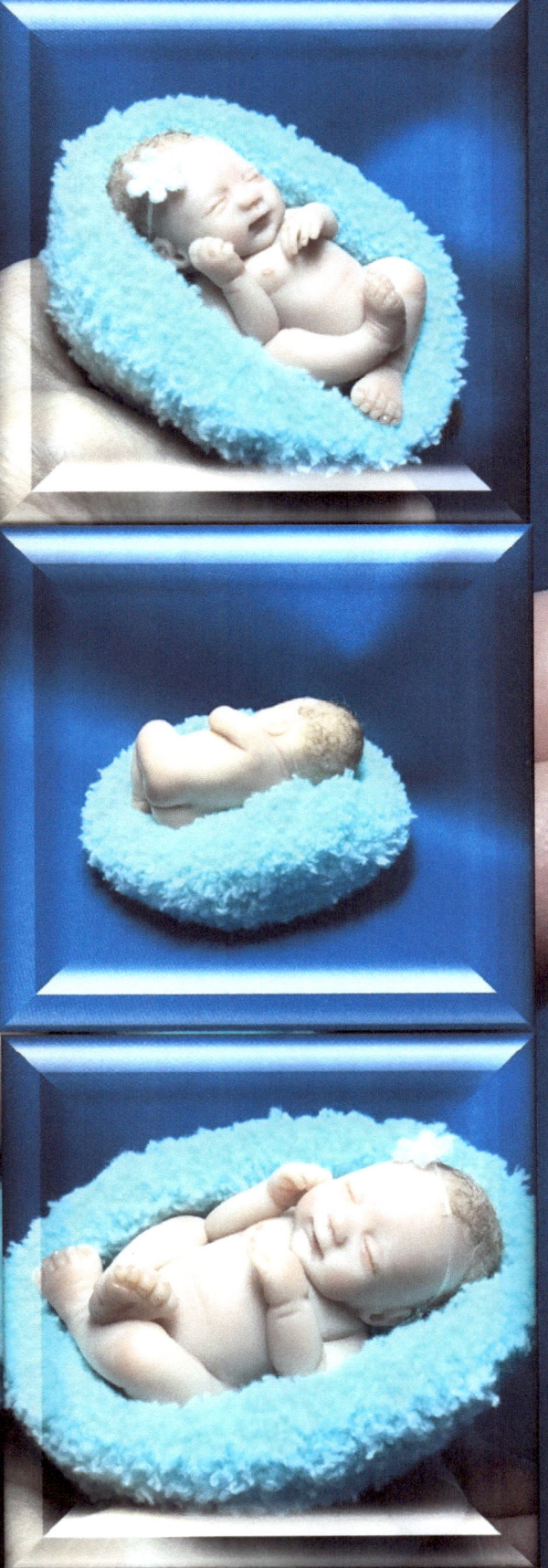

Brenda Scott

Maggie

brendascott1@hotmail.com

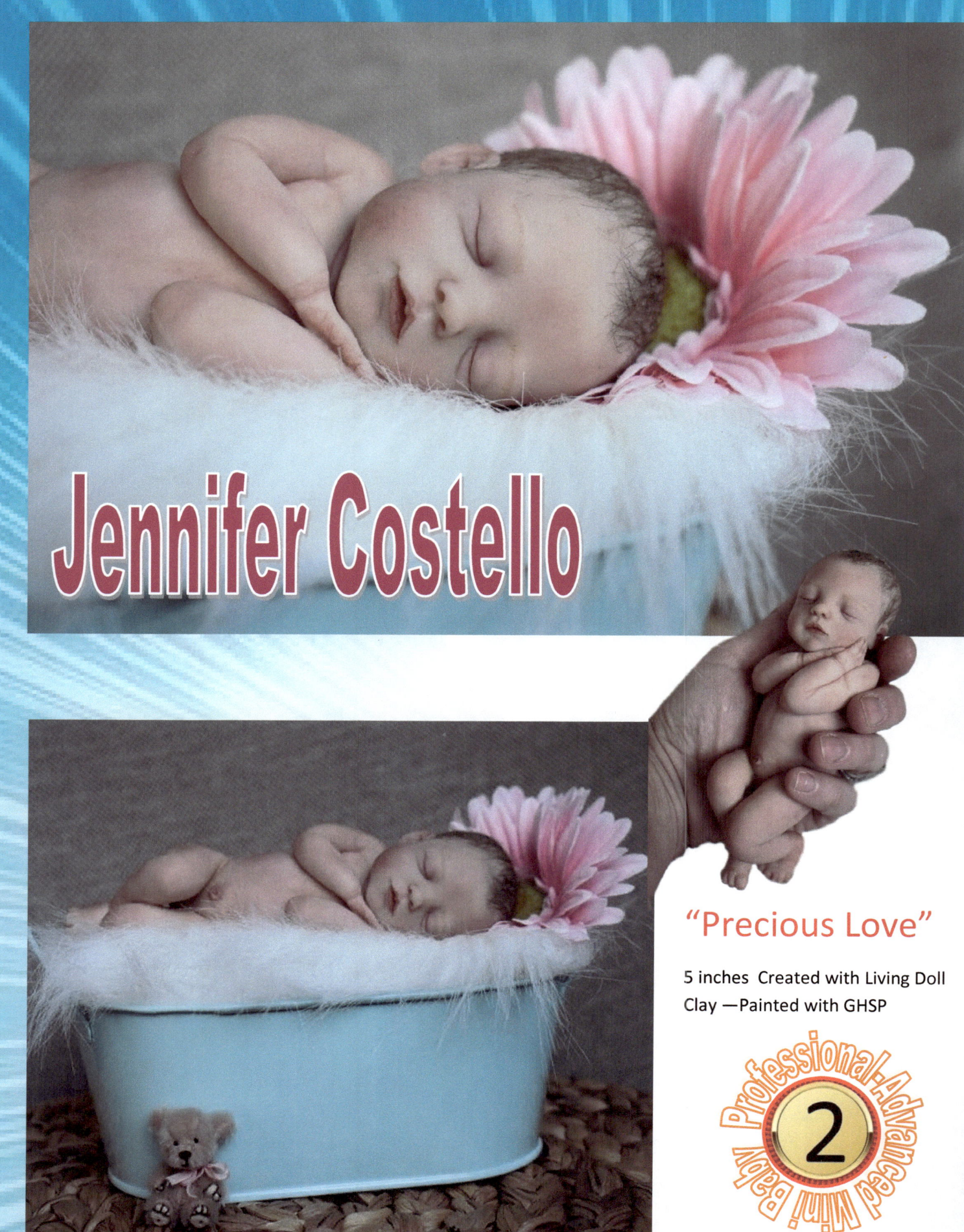

Jennifer Costello

"Precious Love"

5 inches Created with Living Doll Clay —Painted with GHSP

jencost@msn.com

Elsie Rodriquez

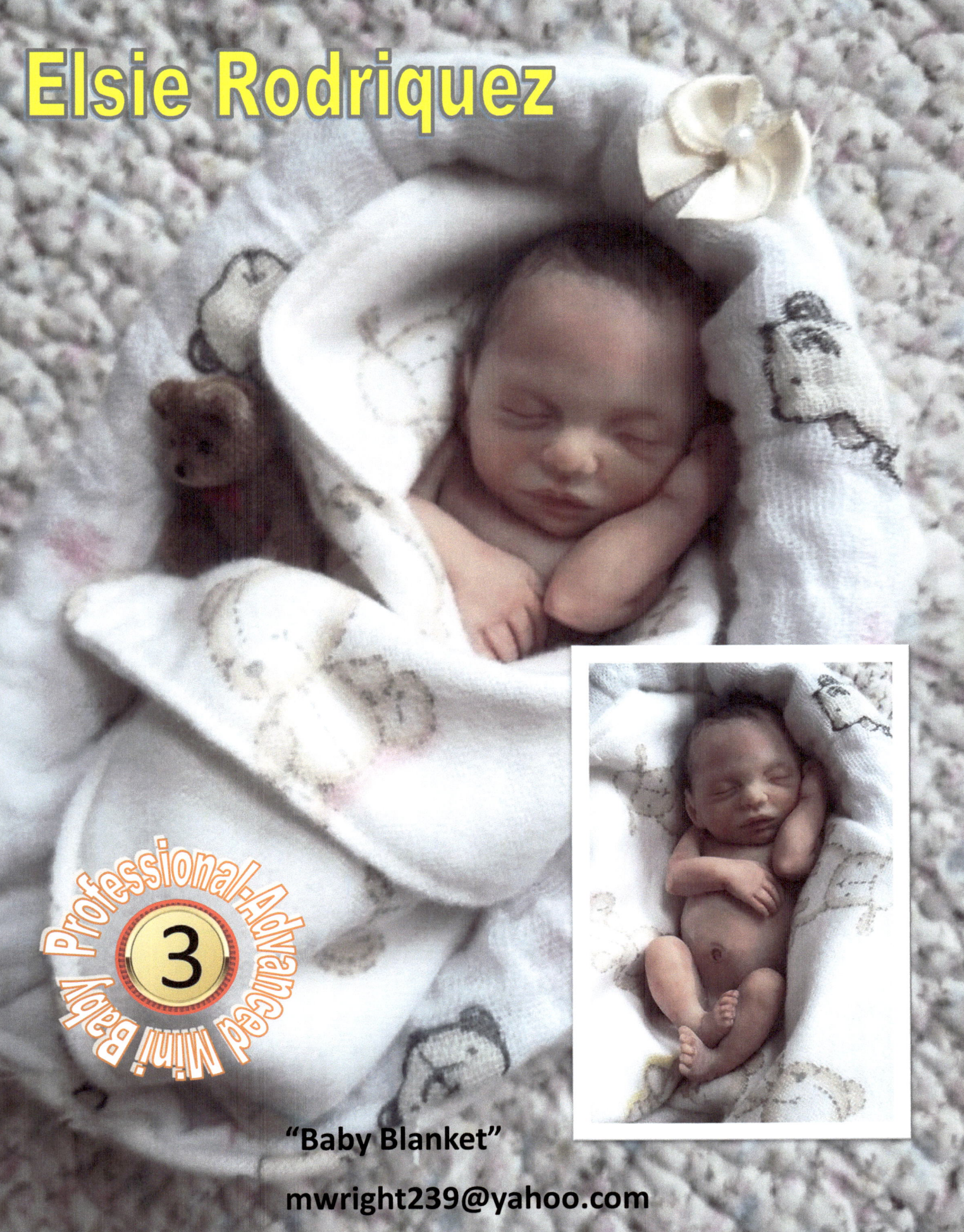

"Baby Blanket"

mwright239@yahoo.com

Anastasia Belova

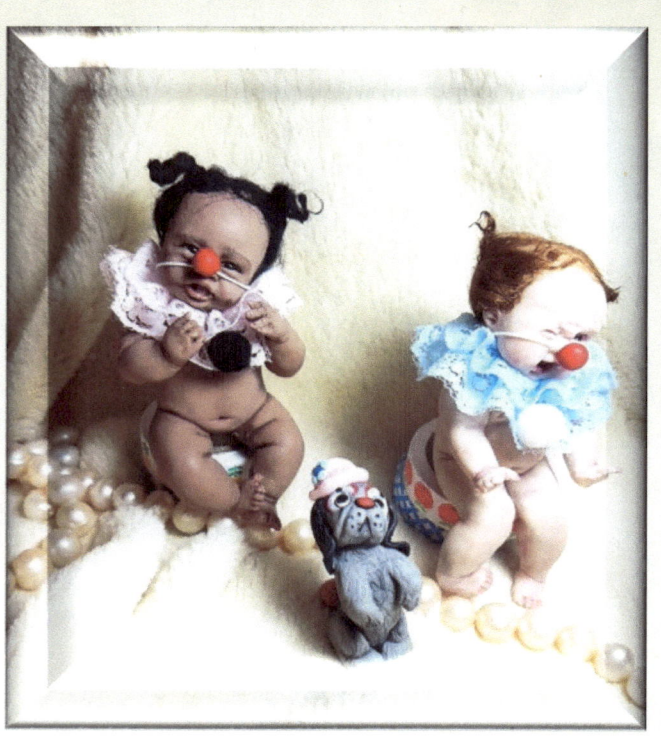
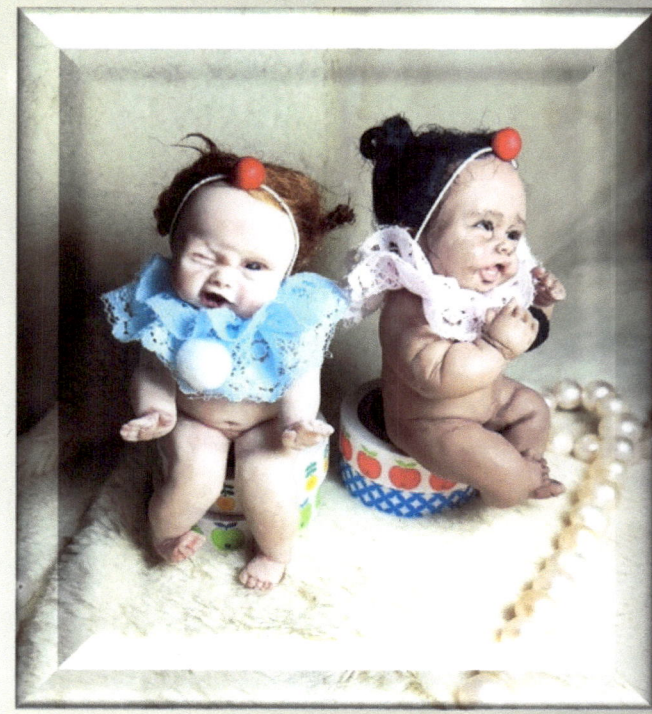

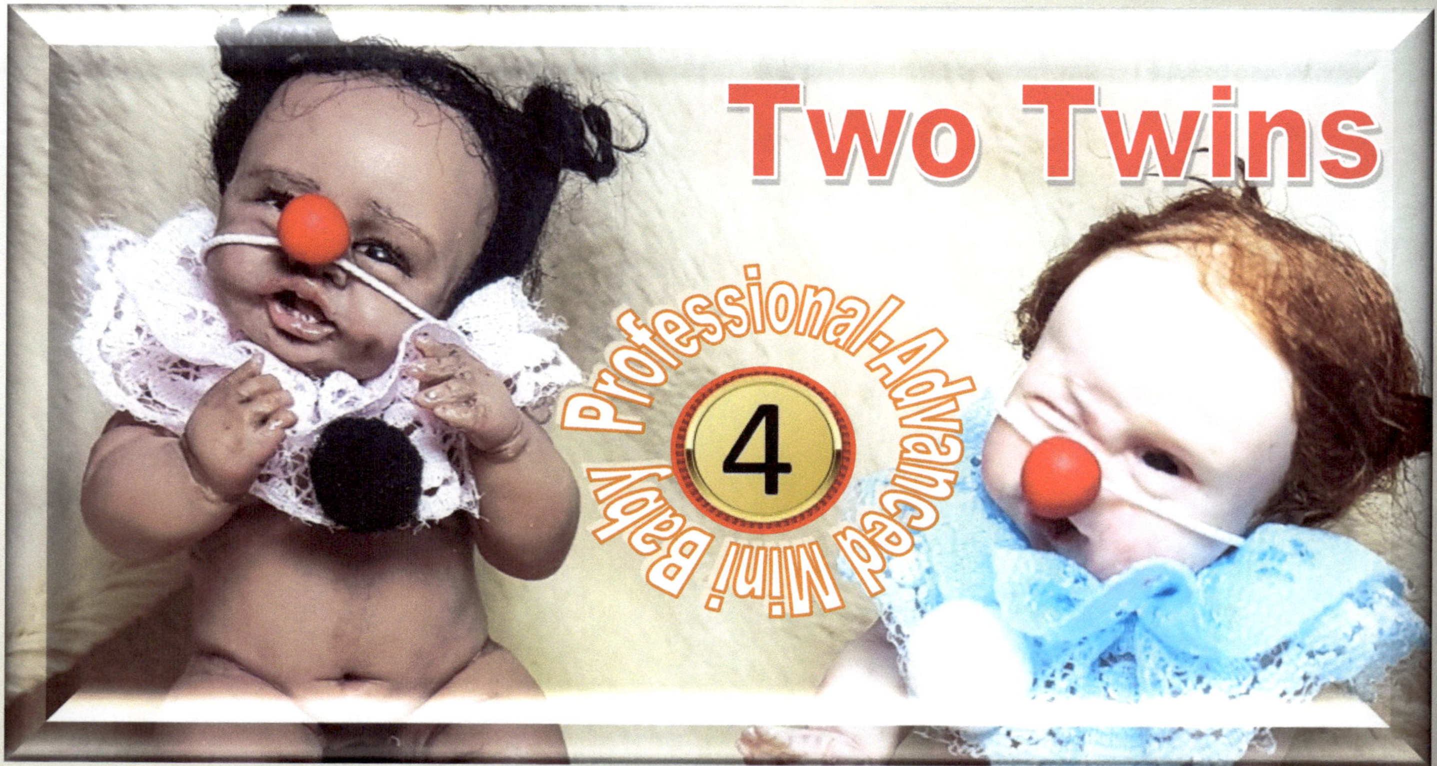

Two Twins

Professional-Advanced Mini Baby 4

"Two twins" The babies are approximately 4 inches size, full sculpted polymer clay OOAK. I used fine English viscose for their hair and painted with a several layers of Genesis heat set paint. The dog is also sculpted by me.

nastitoys@gmail.com

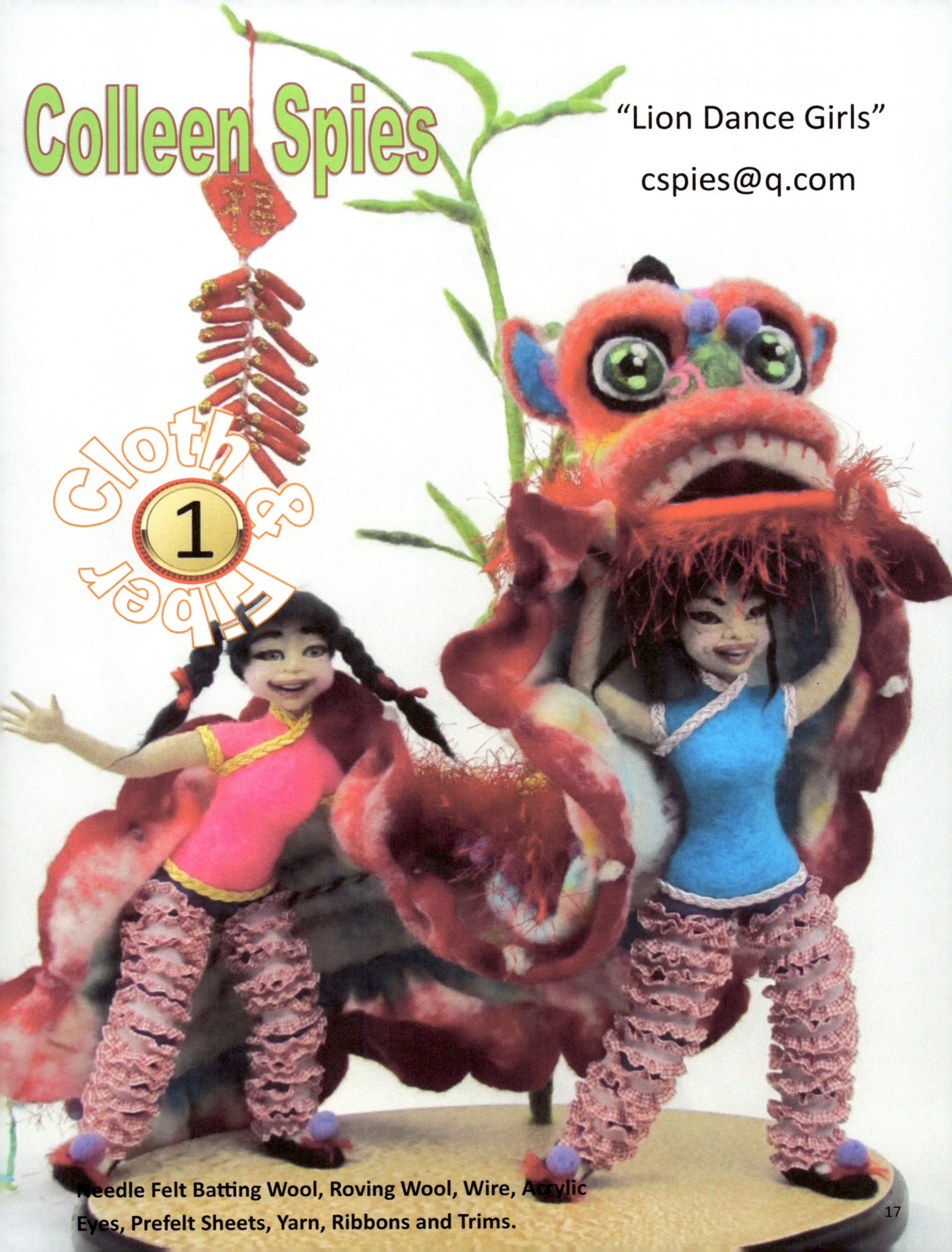

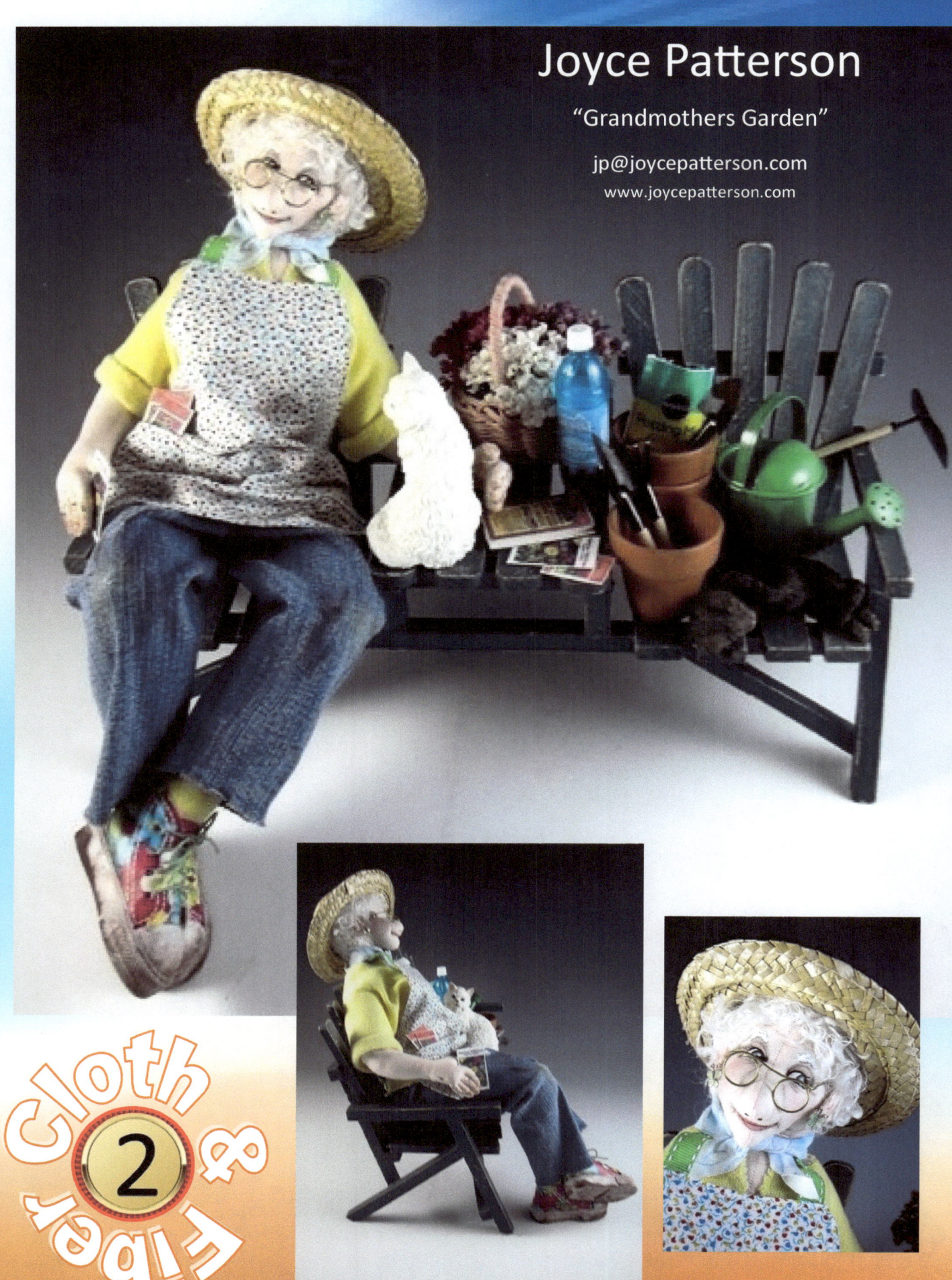

Joyce Patterson

"Grandmothers Garden"

jp@joycepatterson.com
www.joycepatterson.com

June Gallagher

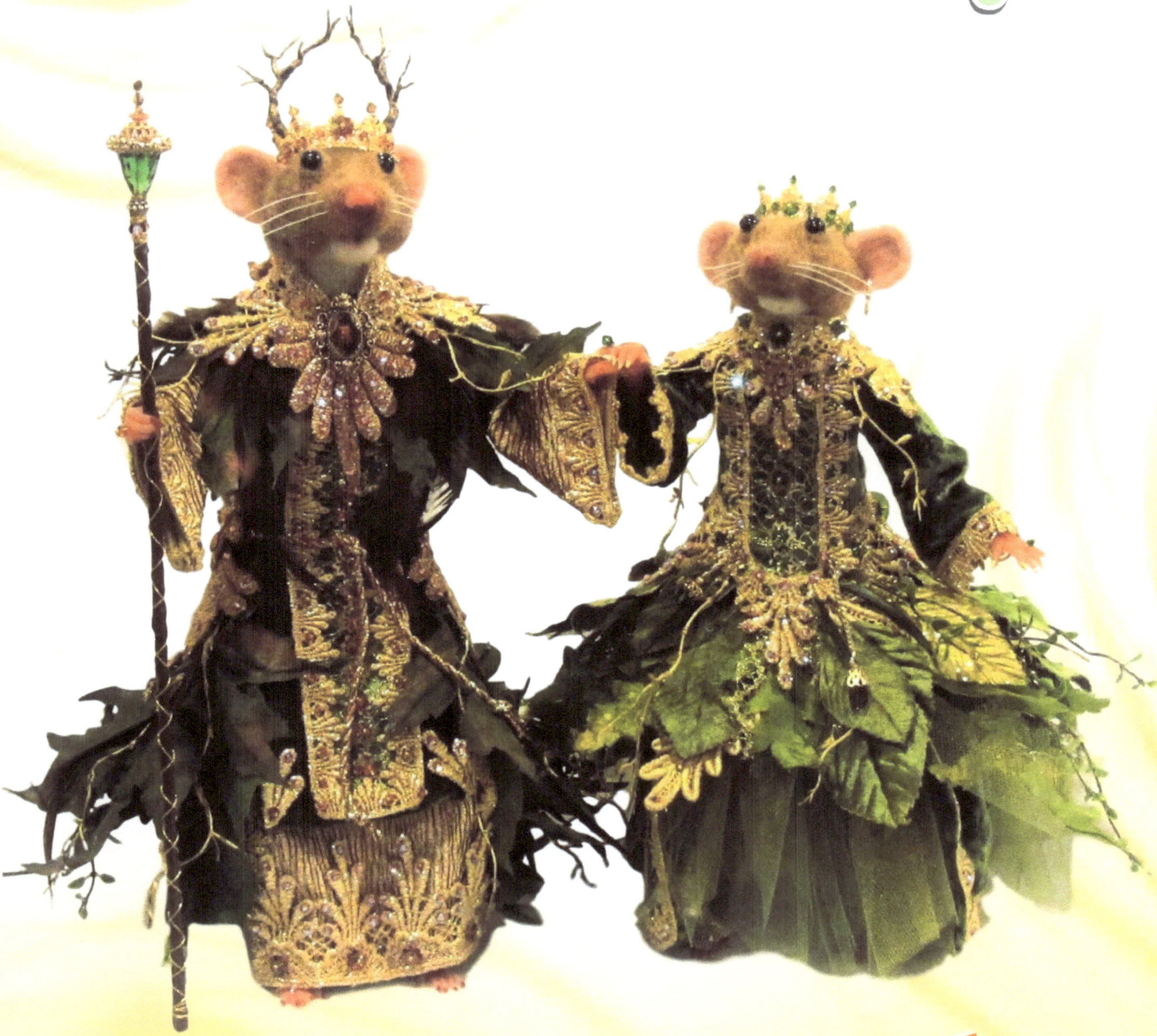

"King Winston and Queen Wilhelmina Woodmouse"

oaknwichlane@gmail.com

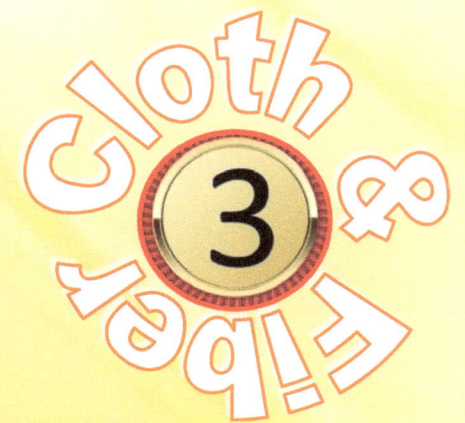

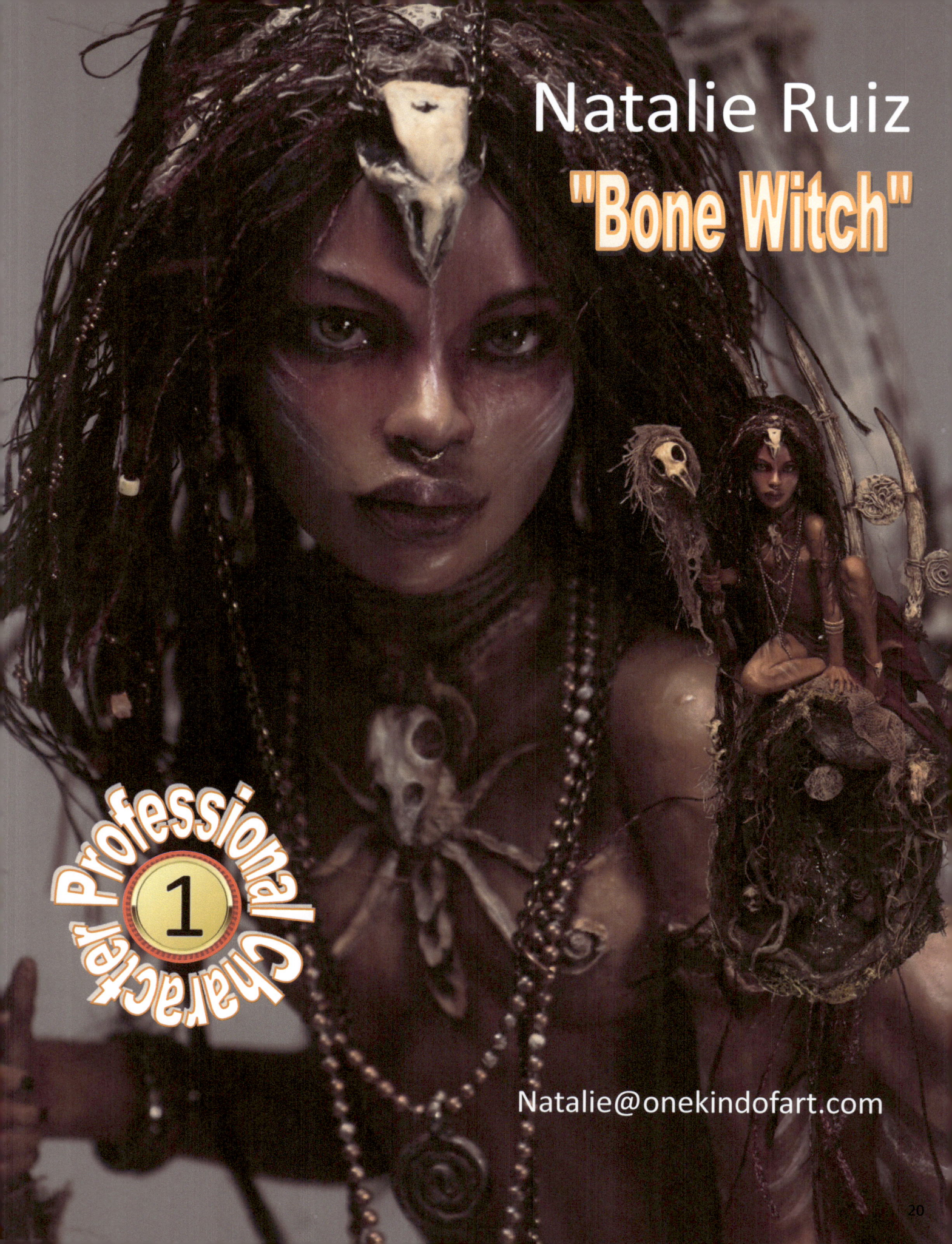

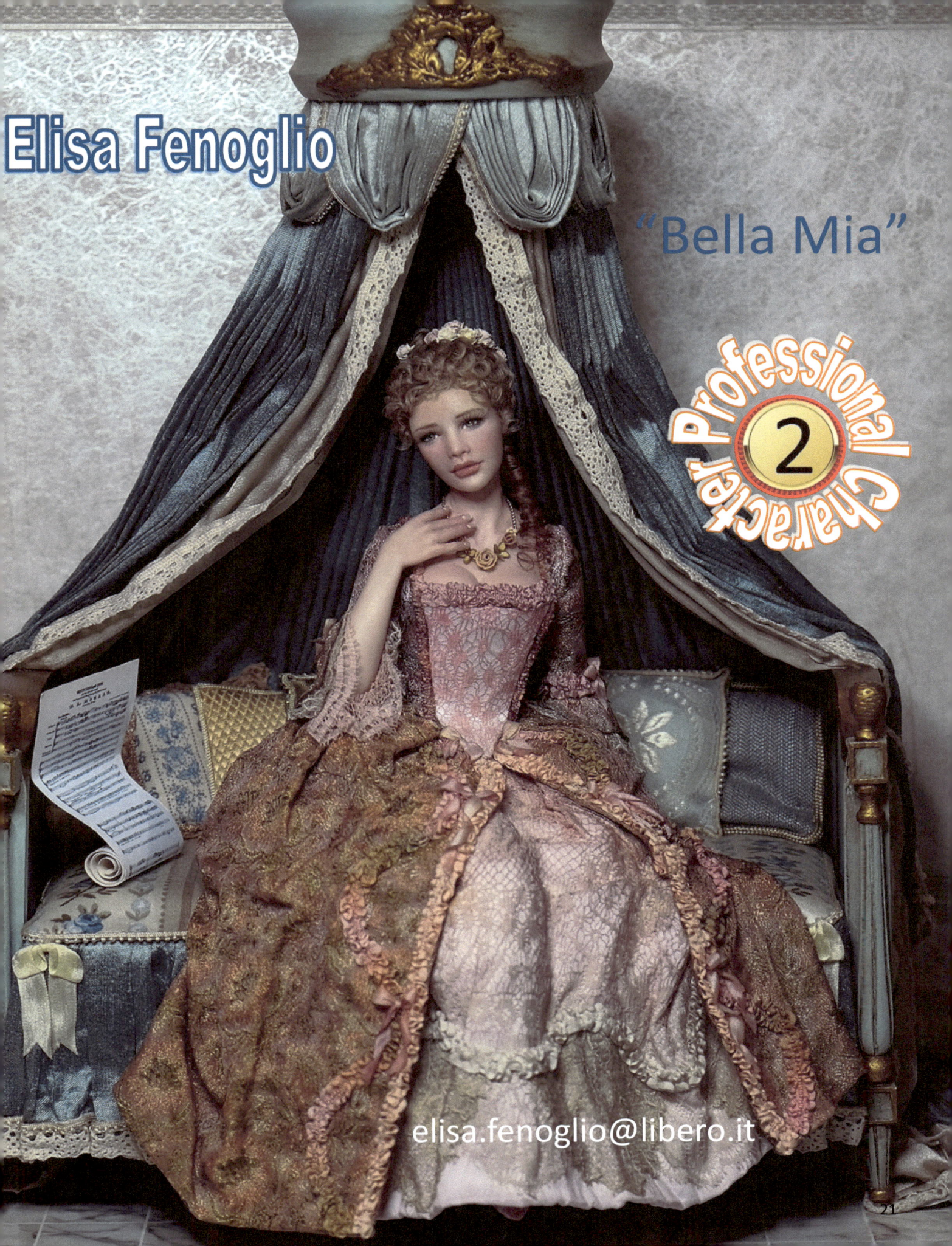

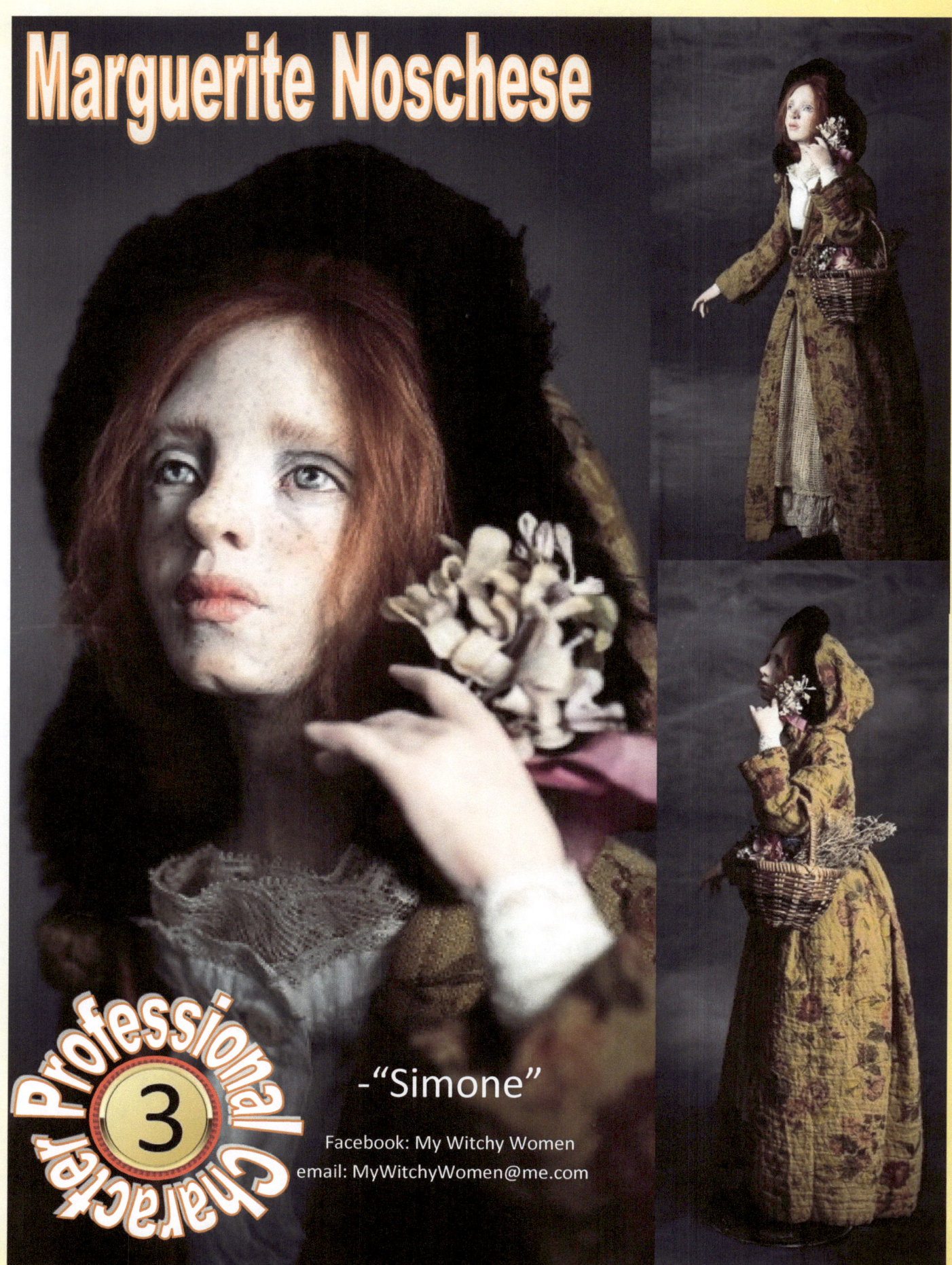

Marguerite Noschese

- "Simone"

Facebook: My Witchy Women
email: MyWitchyWomen@me.com

Professional Character 3

Patrizia Cozzo

Professional Character 4

"White Star"

patriziaeguido@mac.com

Esther Manso

"Ghost of Christmas Past"

techymanso@gmail.com

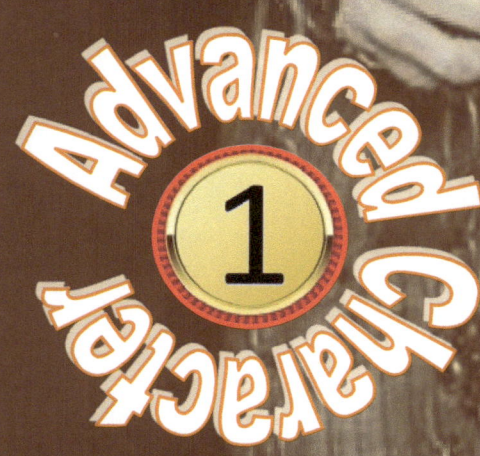

Michelle Pulaski

"Light Bringer Knome"

Realms06@hotmail.com

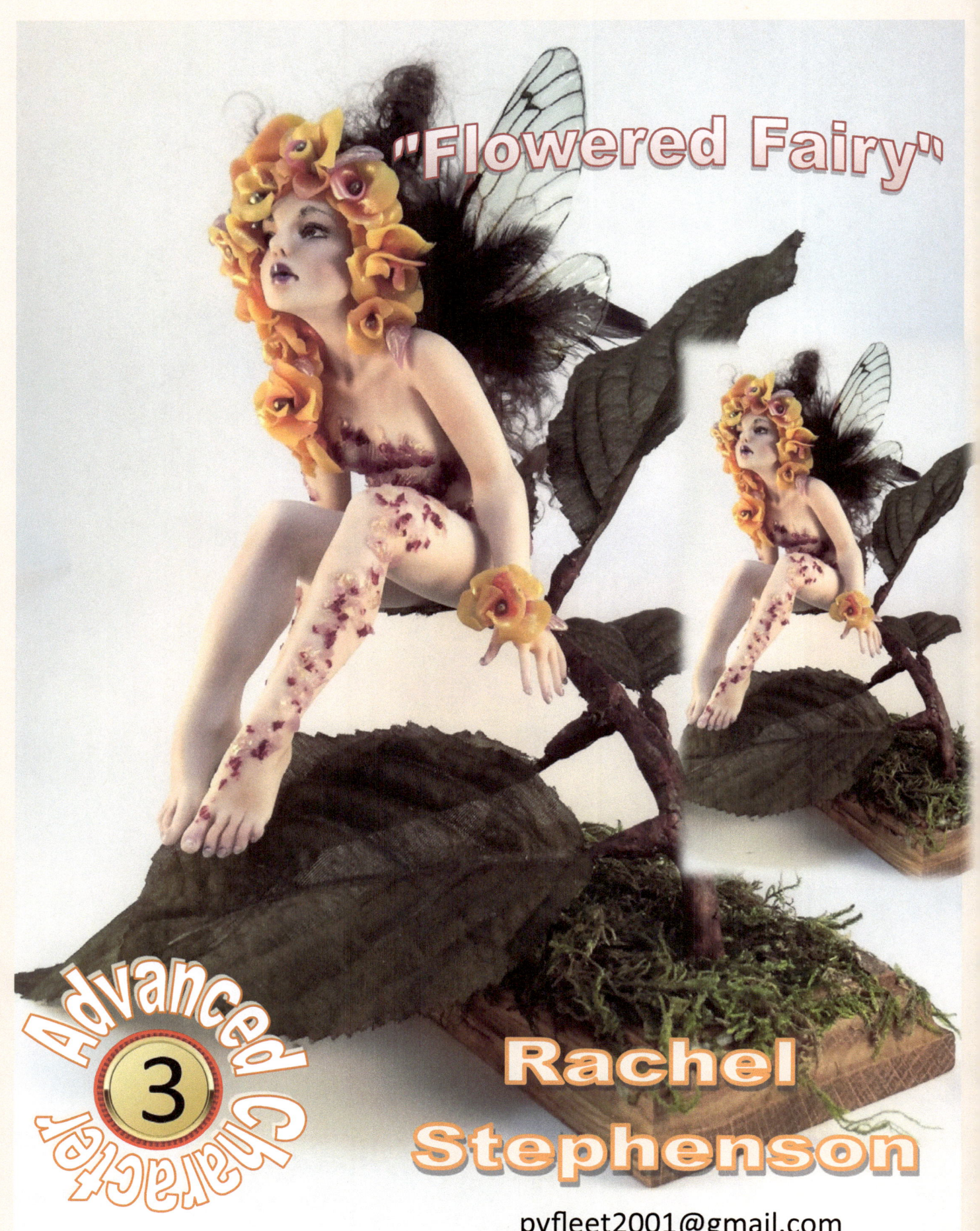

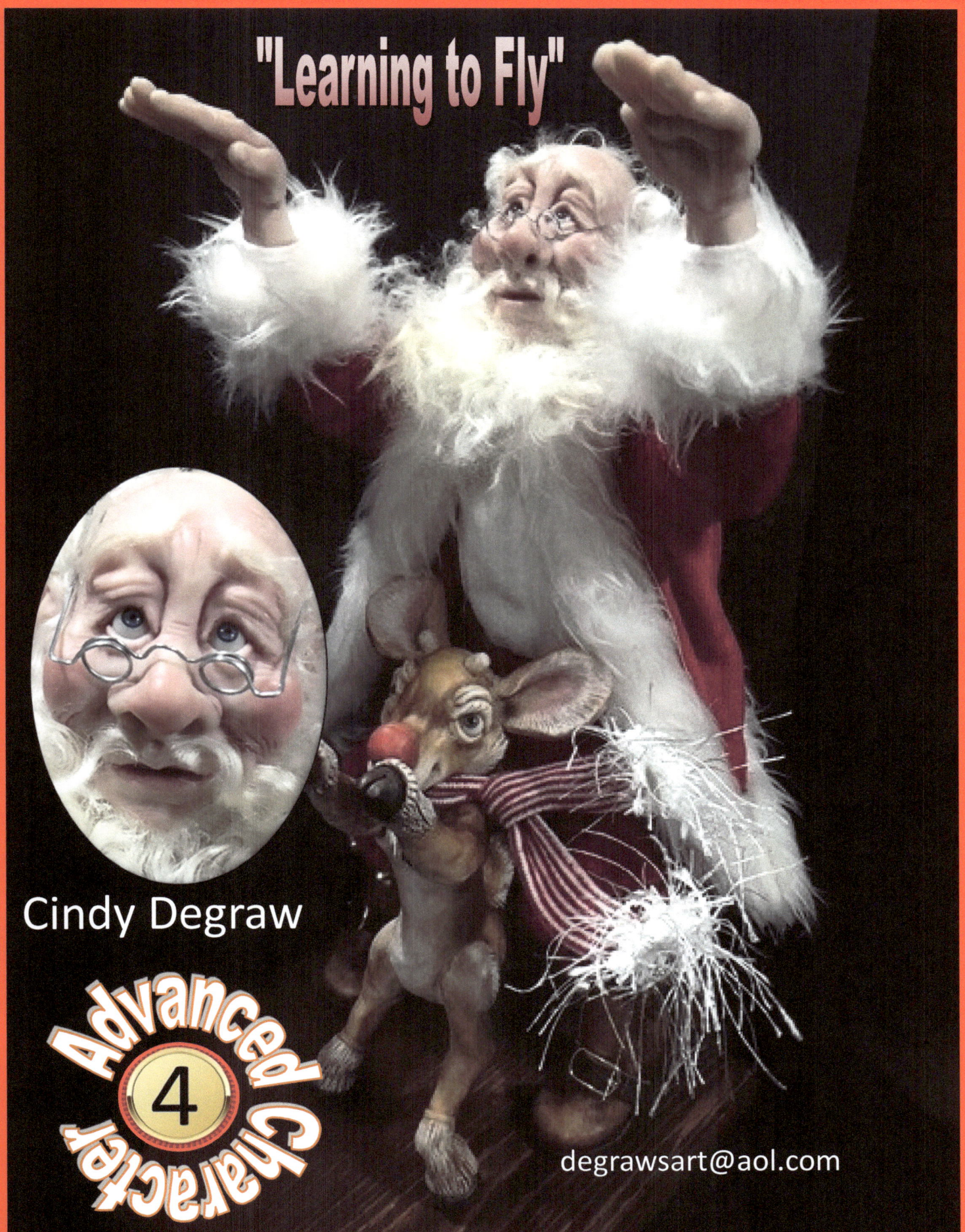

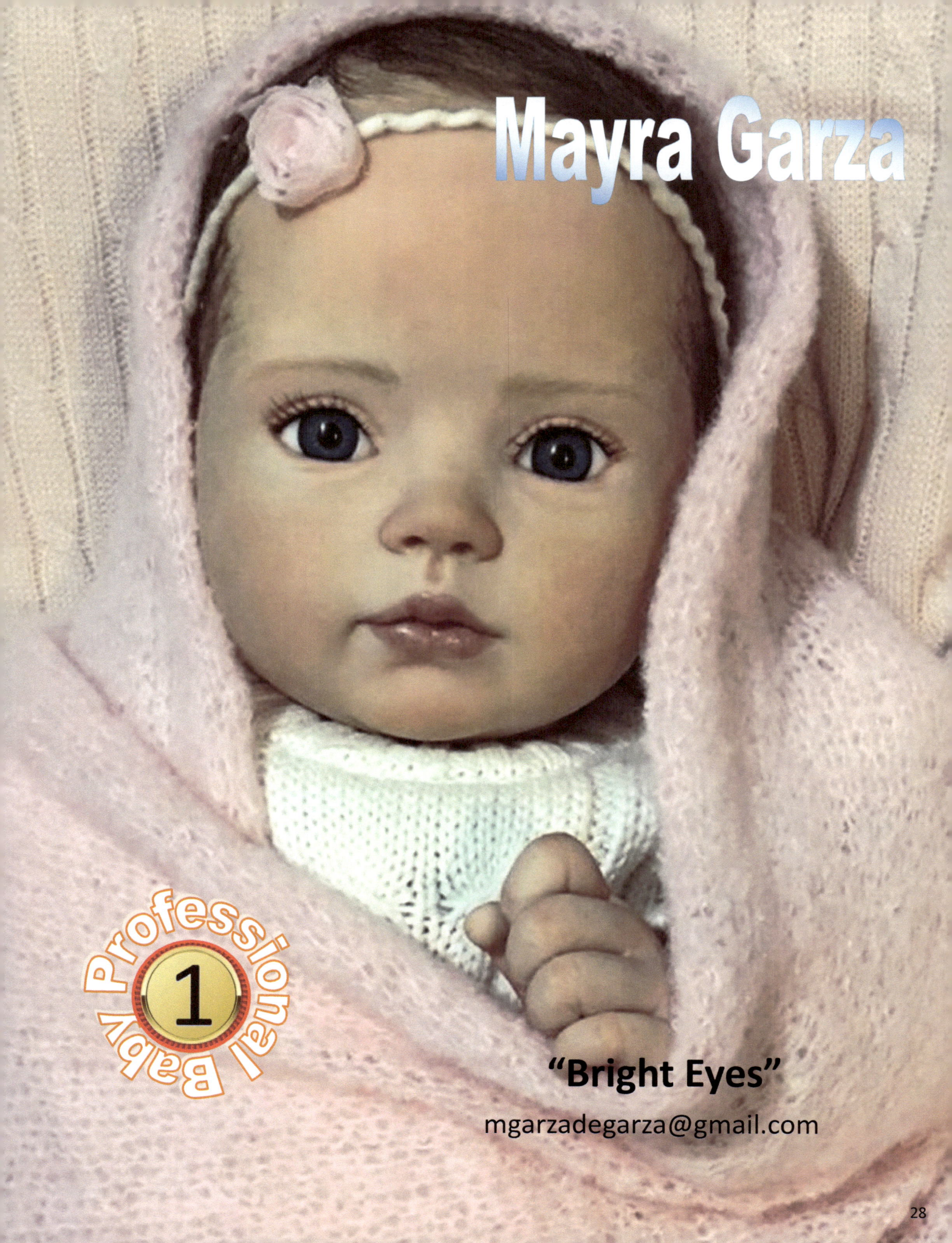

"Bright Eyes"
mgarzadegarza@gmail.com

Sherri Williams

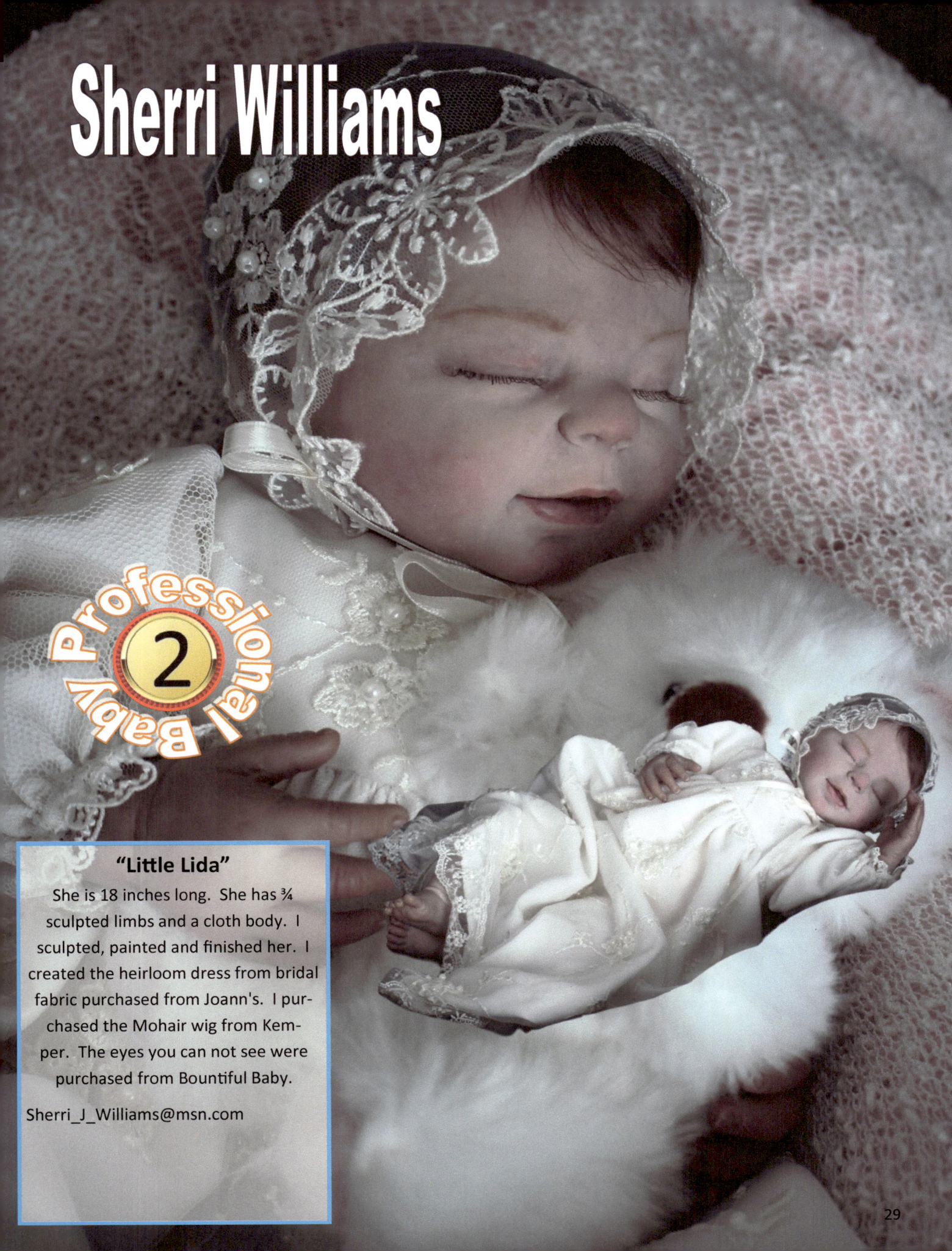

"Little Lida"

She is 18 inches long. She has ¾ sculpted limbs and a cloth body. I sculpted, painted and finished her. I created the heirloom dress from bridal fabric purchased from Joann's. I purchased the Mohair wig from Kemper. The eyes you can not see were purchased from Bountiful Baby.

Sherri_J_Williams@msn.com

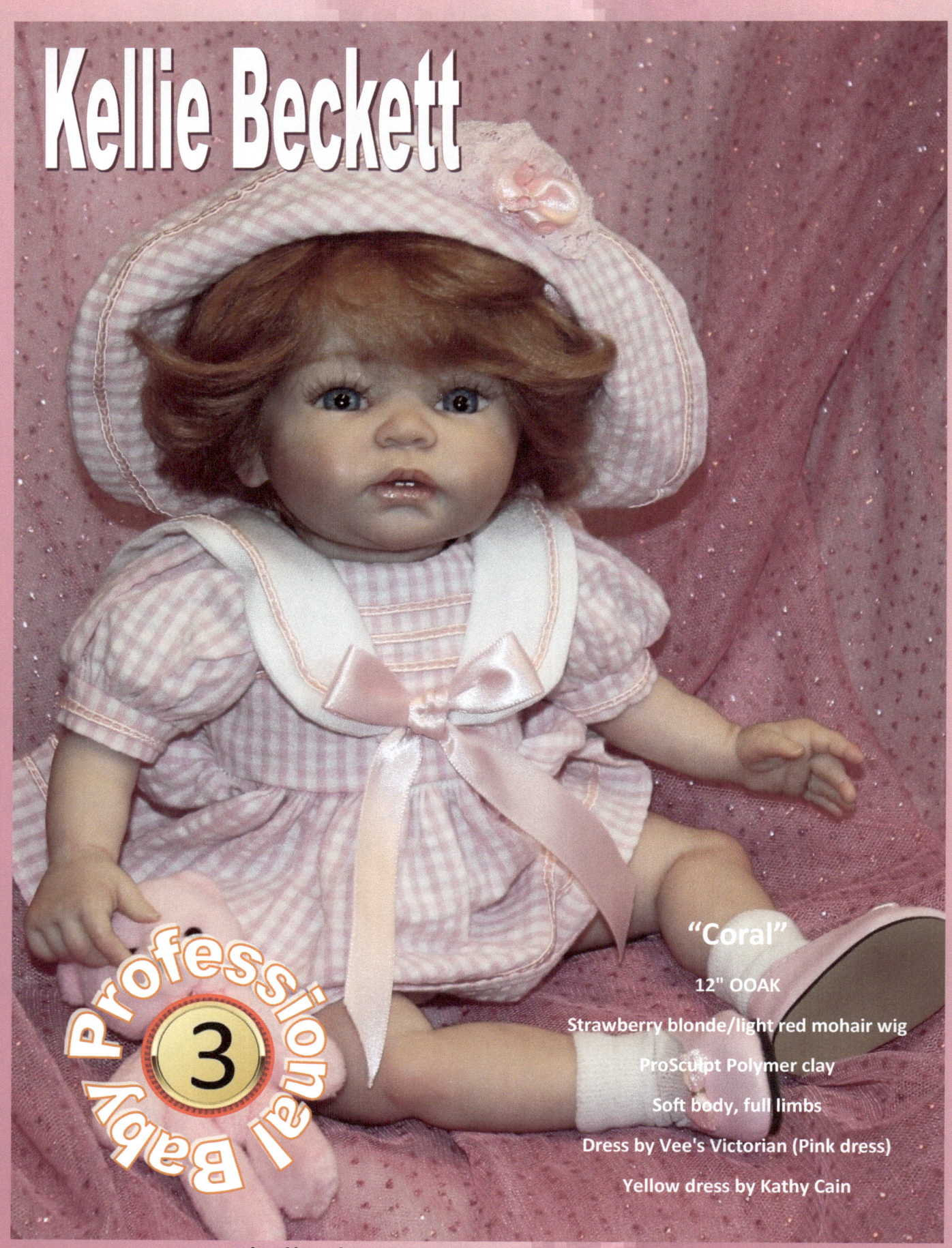

Kellie Beckett

"Coral"

12" OOAK

Strawberry blonde/light red mohair wig

ProSculpt Polymer clay

Soft body, full limbs

Dress by Vee's Victorian (Pink dress)

Yellow dress by Kathy Cain

kellie.beckett@gmail.com

Hope Mason

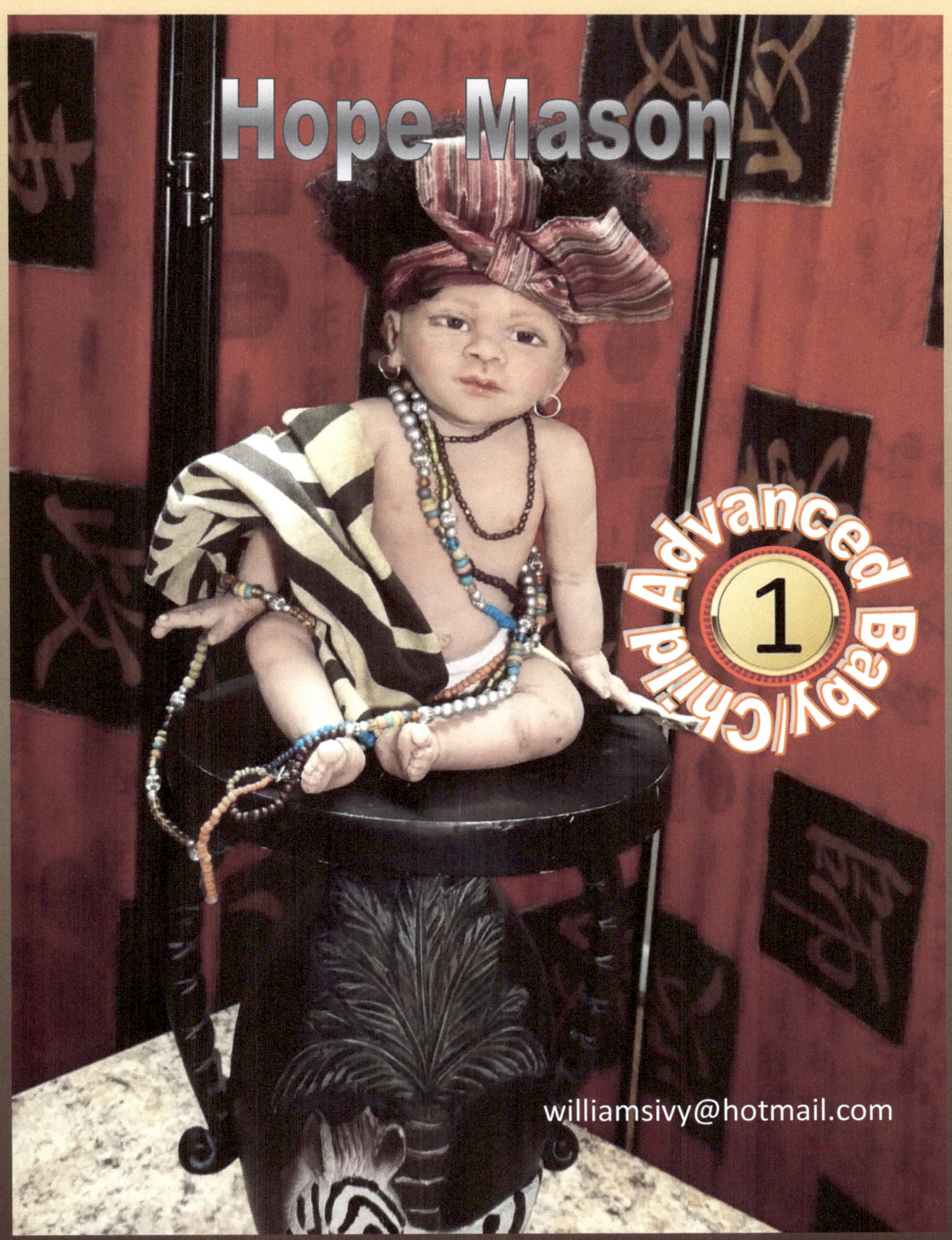

williamsivy@hotmail.com

"Baby beads"

Baby Rhia Polymer Clay

6 inches sitting African Princess

Jan Wright

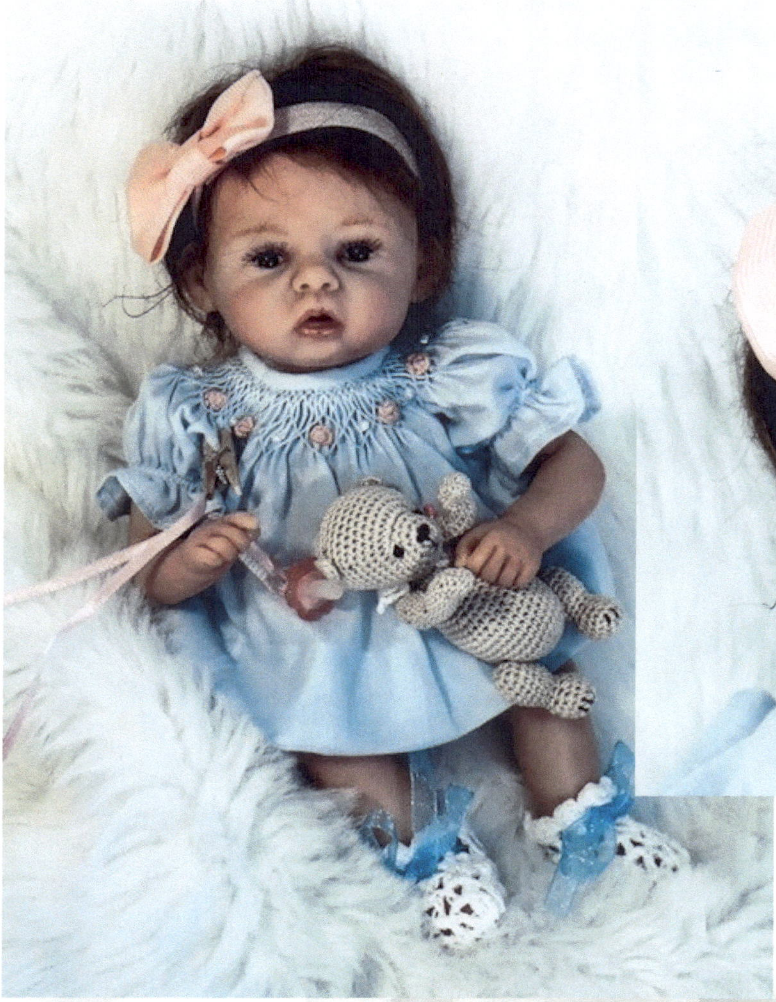

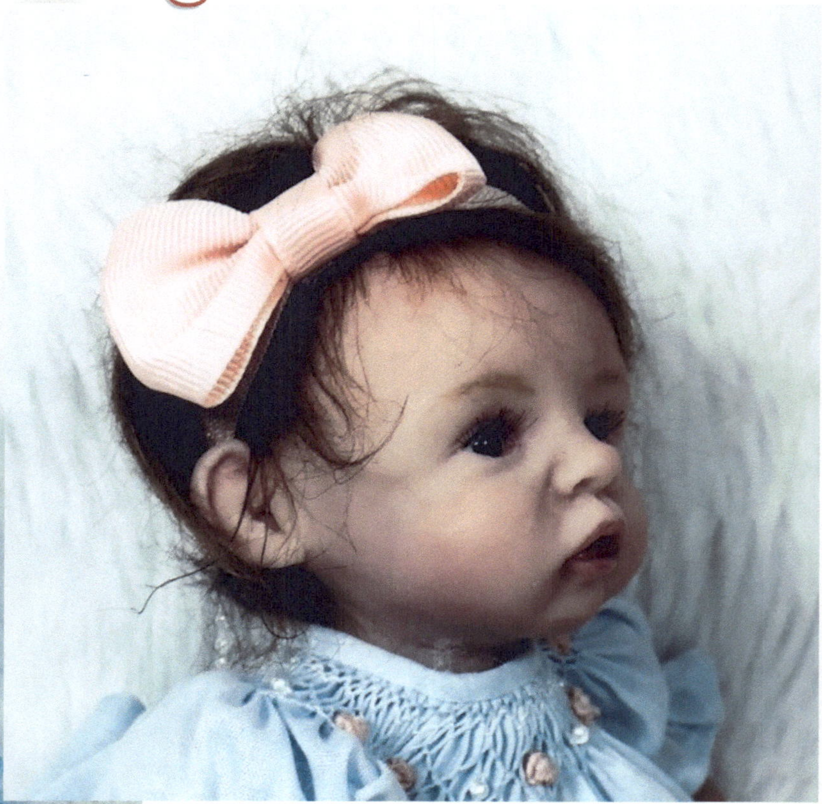

"Janey Marie"

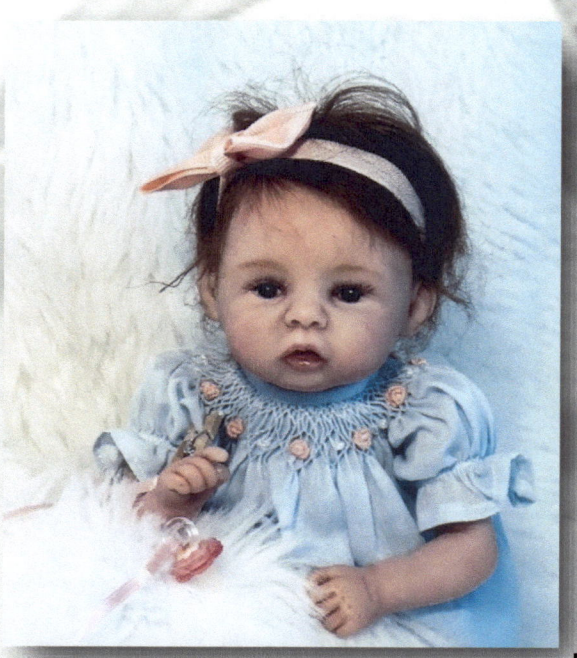
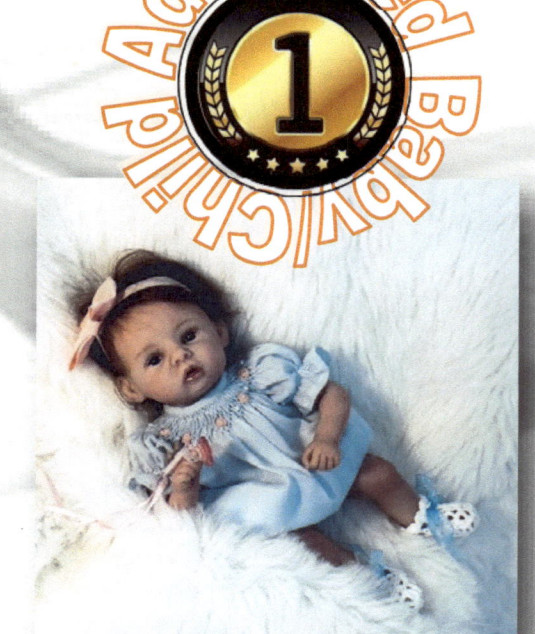

Janwright00@gmail.com

Peggy McChesney

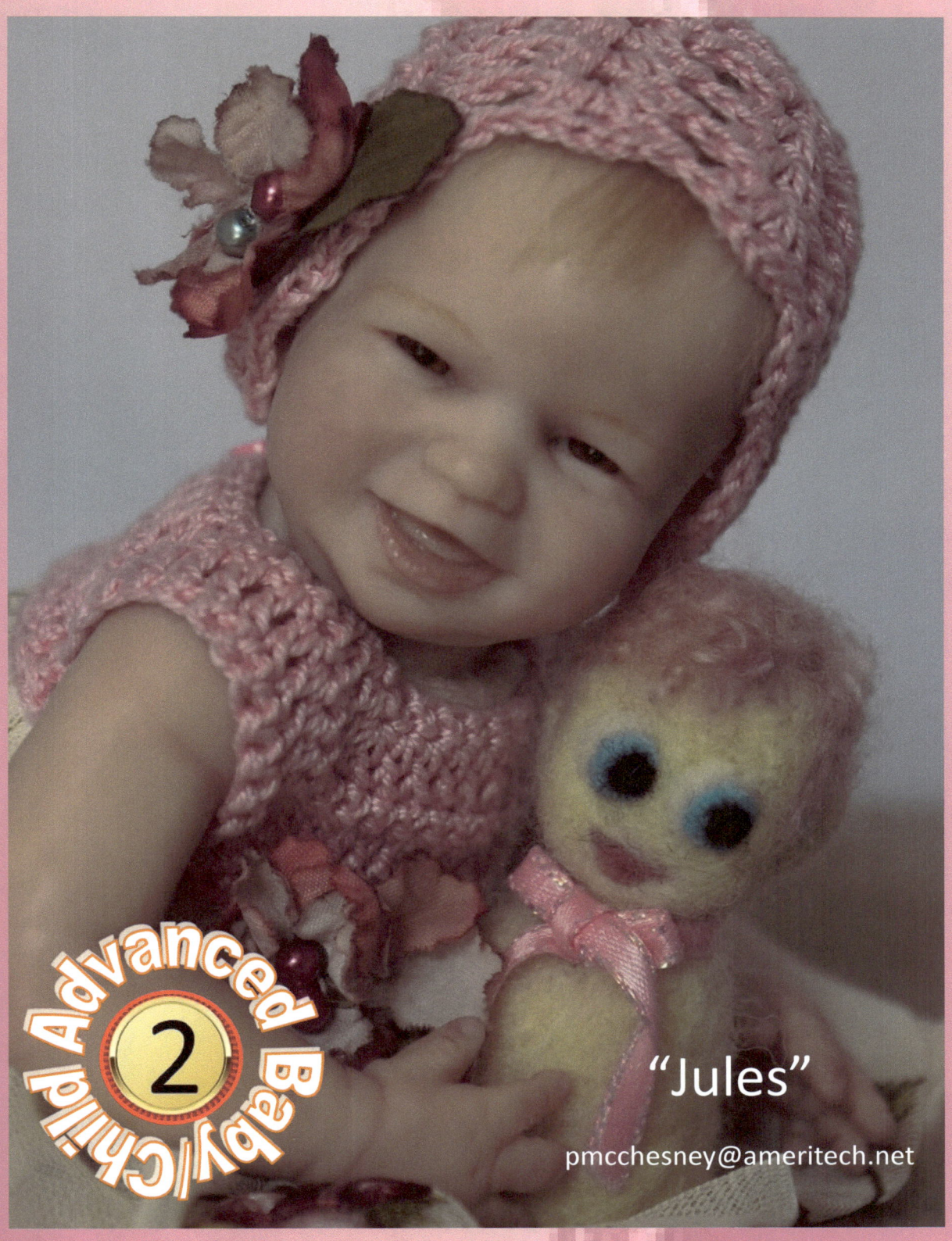

"Jules"

pmcchesney@ameritech.net

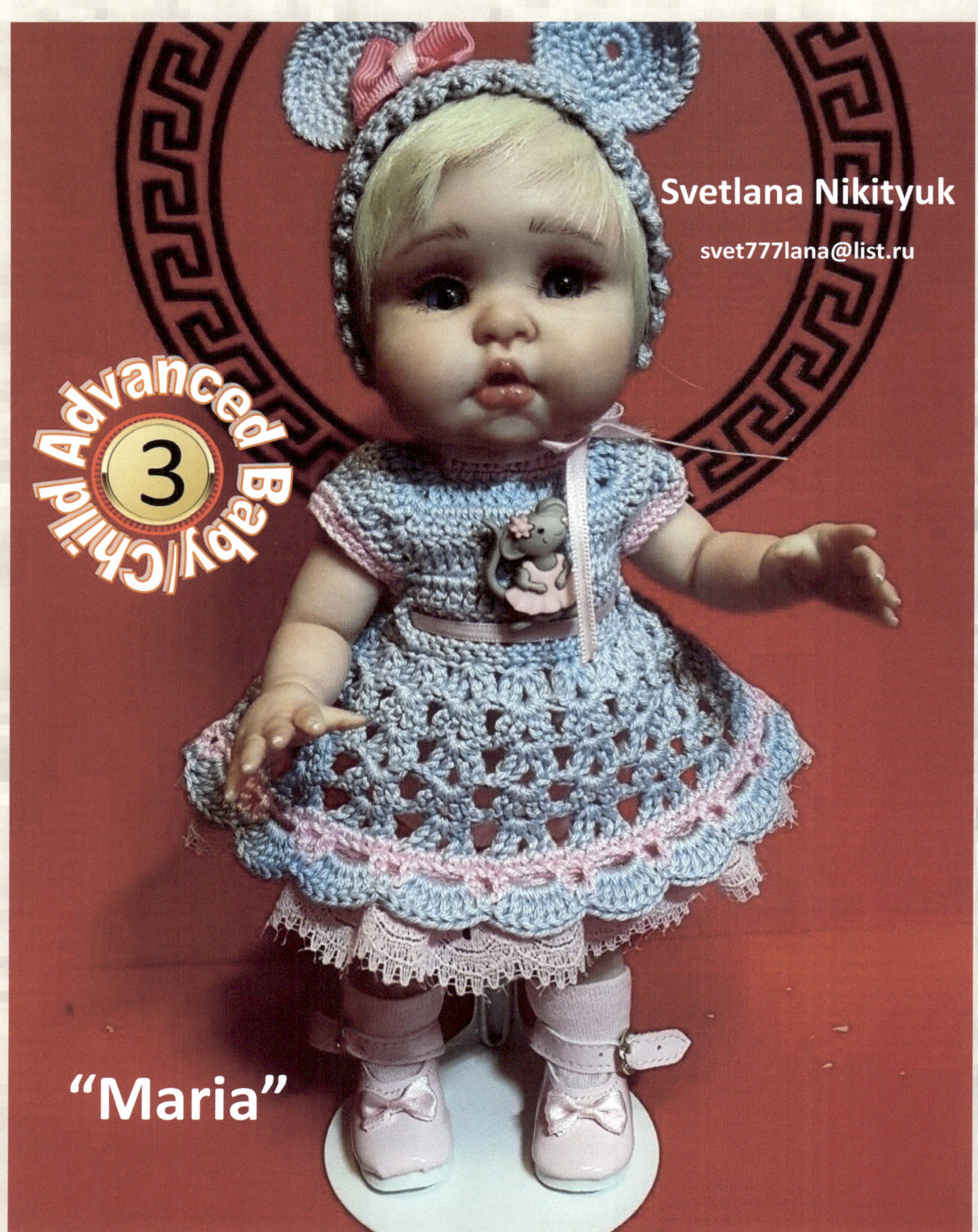

Mary Ann Banish

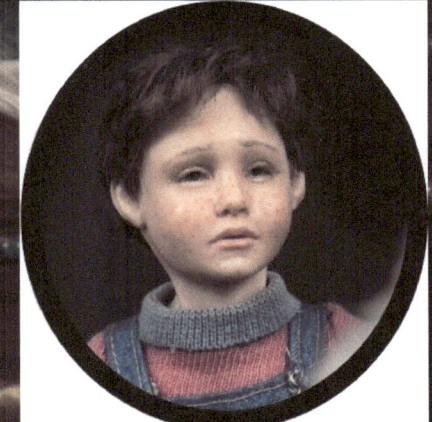

Intermediate 1

"Santa and Cody"

mabanish@gmail.com

Elisabetta Visentini

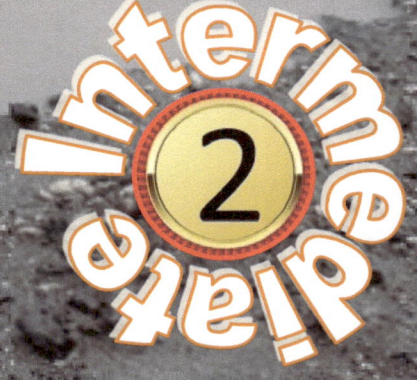

"Araknofolie"

elisabetta.visentini@gmail.com

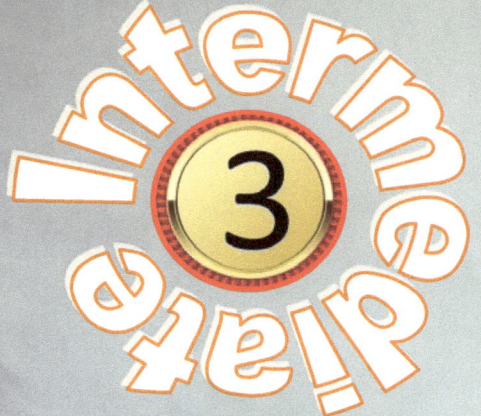

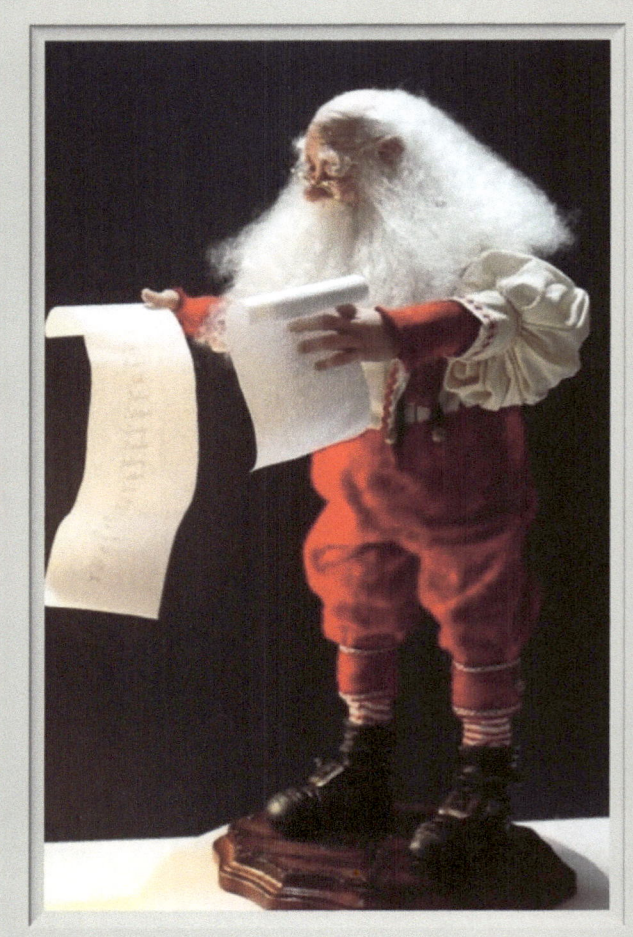

Sherrie Nielson

"Santa Checking List"

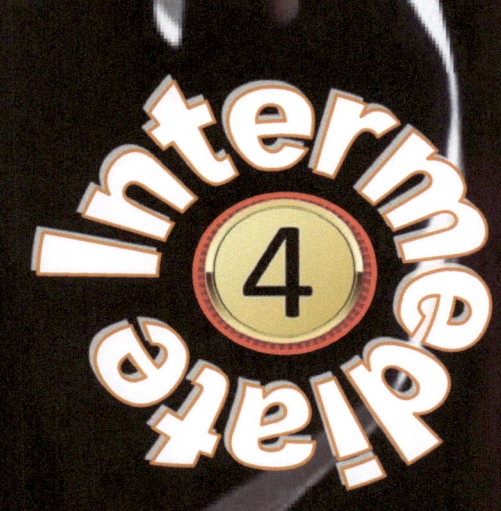

sherrineilson@yahoo.com

Jennifer Abel

"Jim Fishing"

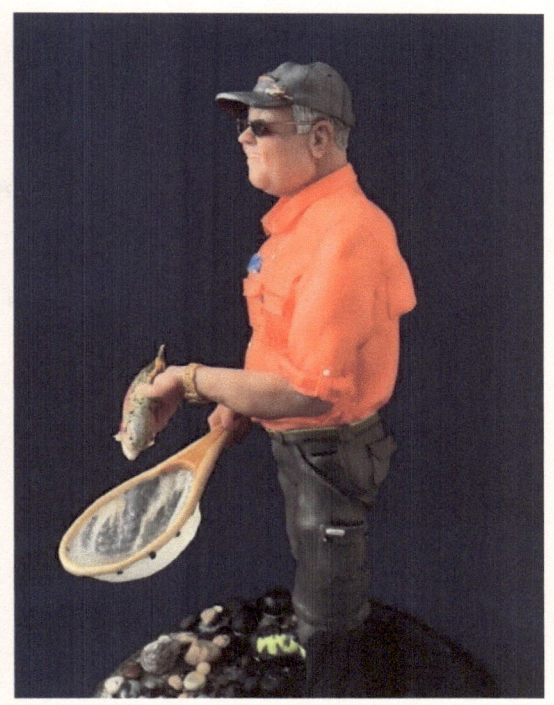
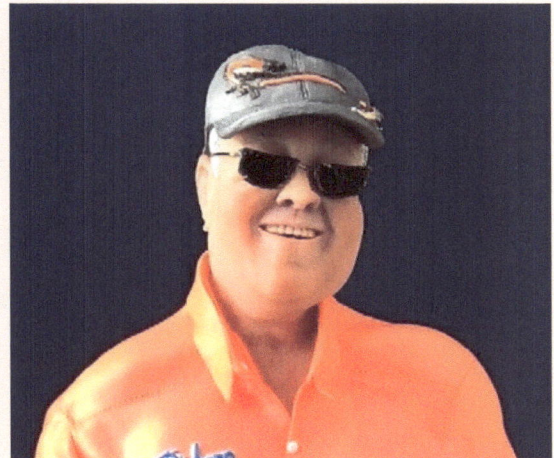
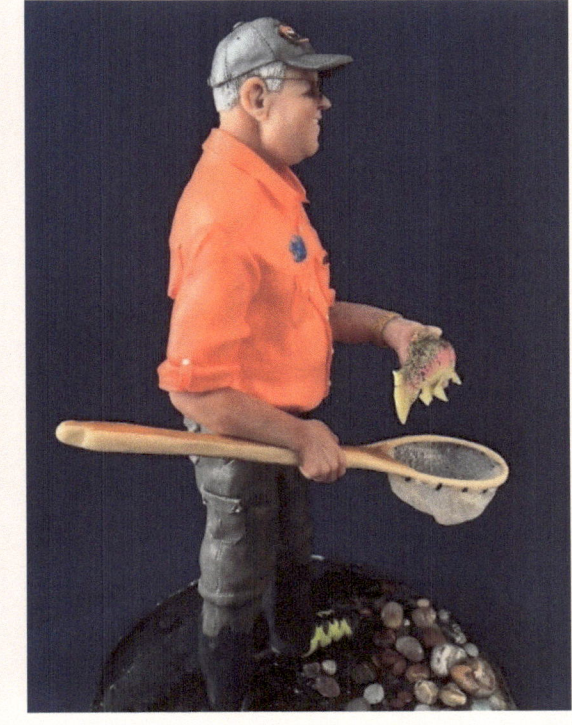

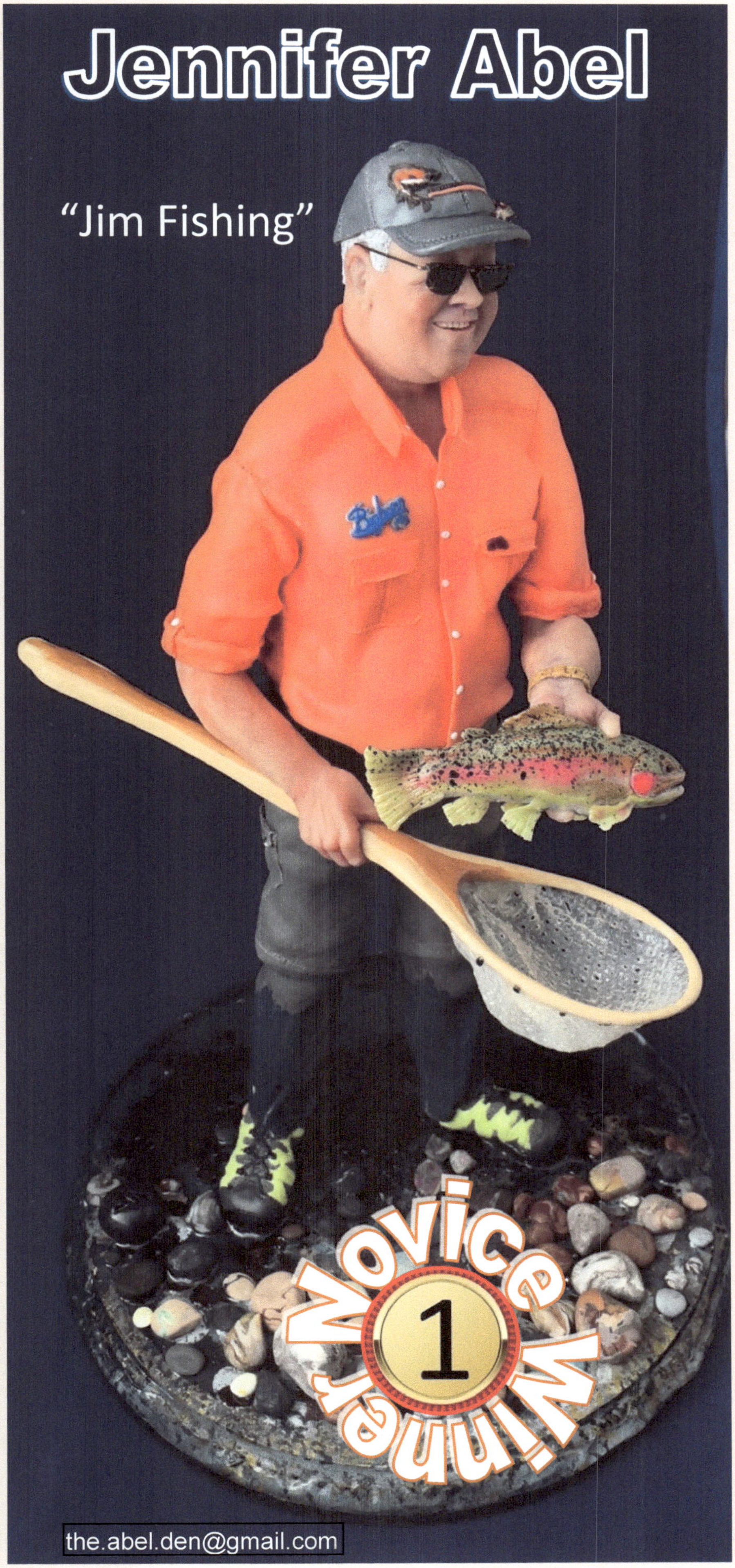

Novice Winner 1

the.abel.den@gmail.com

Barbara Cintolesi

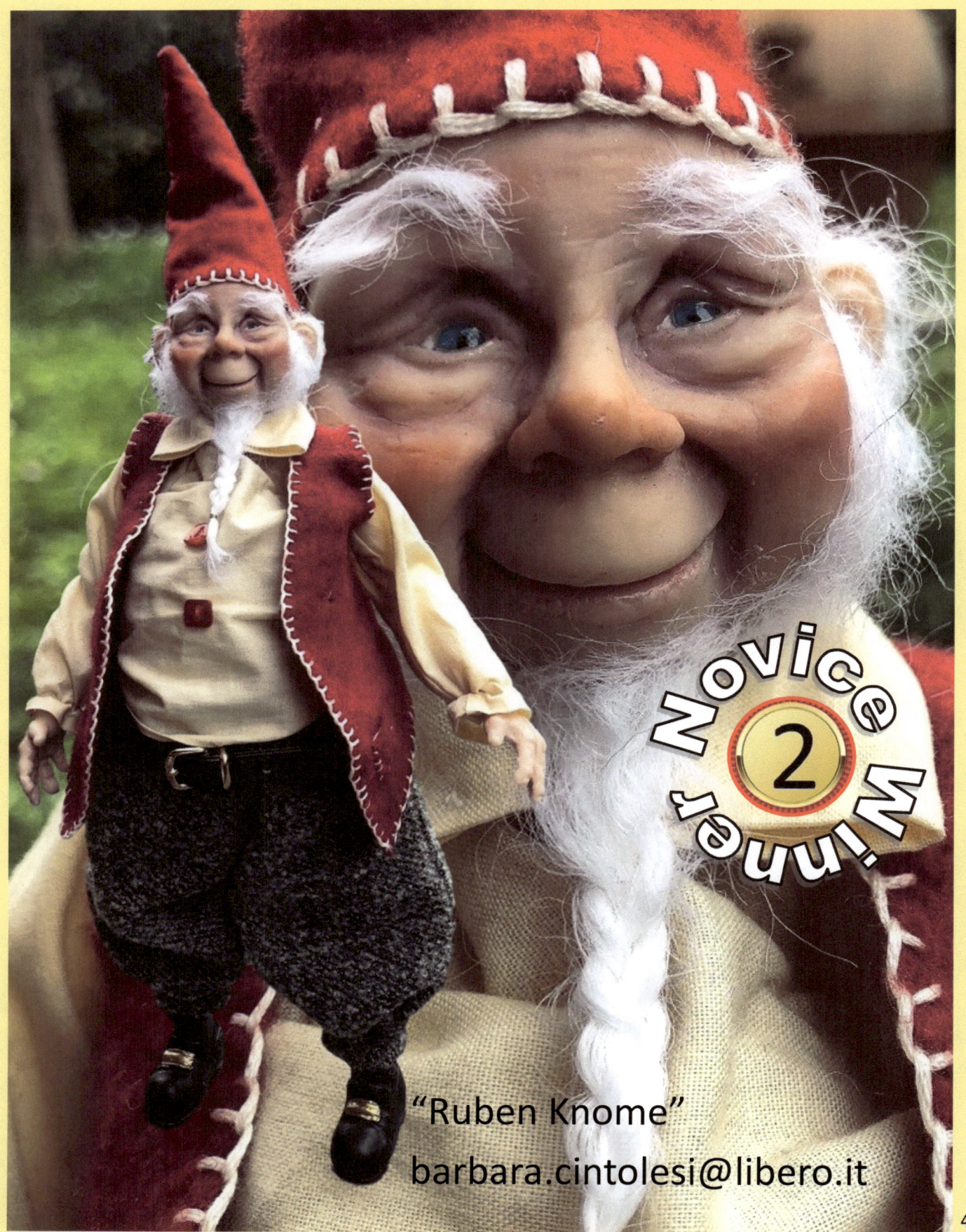

Novice Winner 2

"Ruben Knome"
barbara.cintolesi@libero.it

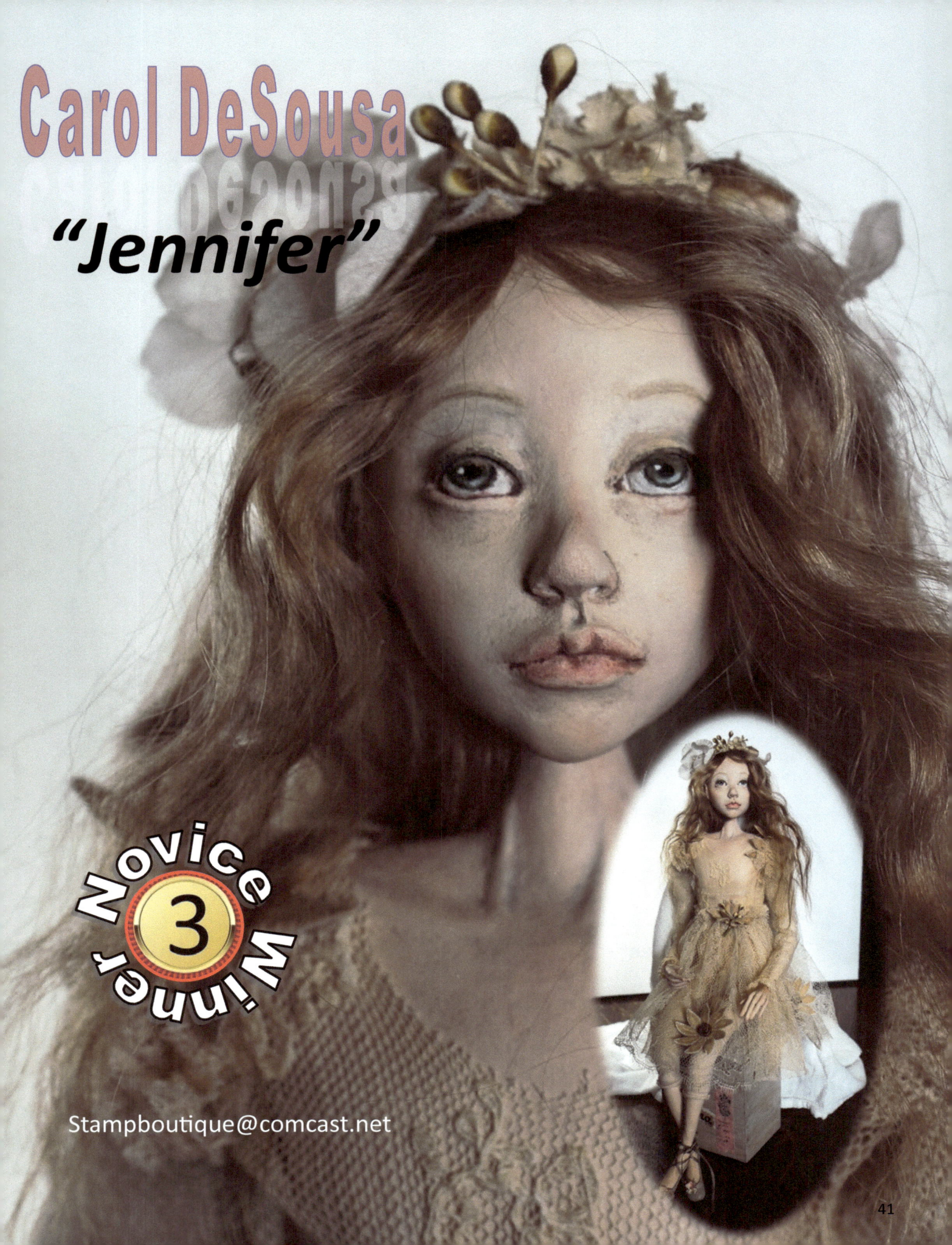

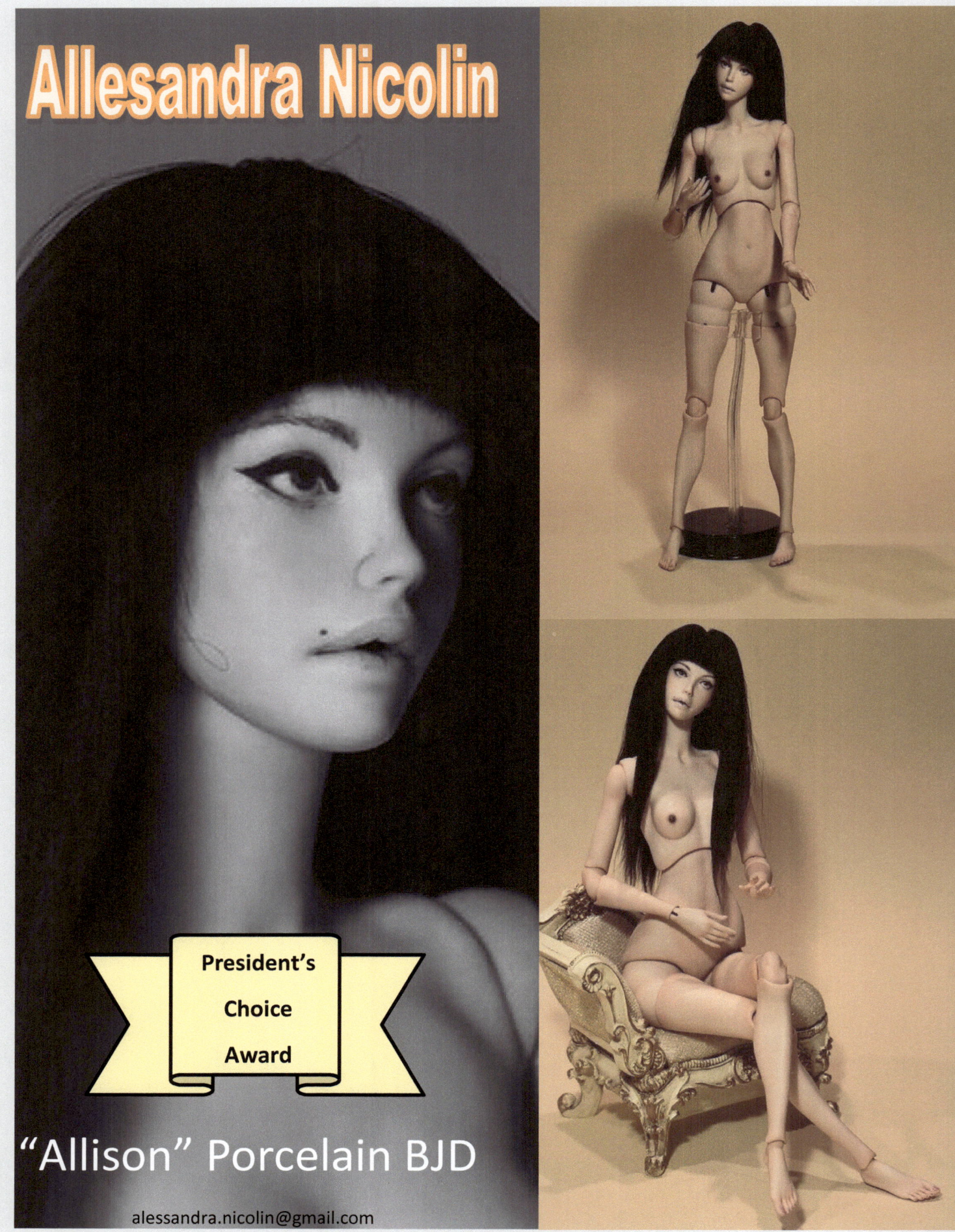

Allesandra Nicolin

President's Choice Award

"Allison" Porcelain BJD

alessandra.nicolin@gmail.com

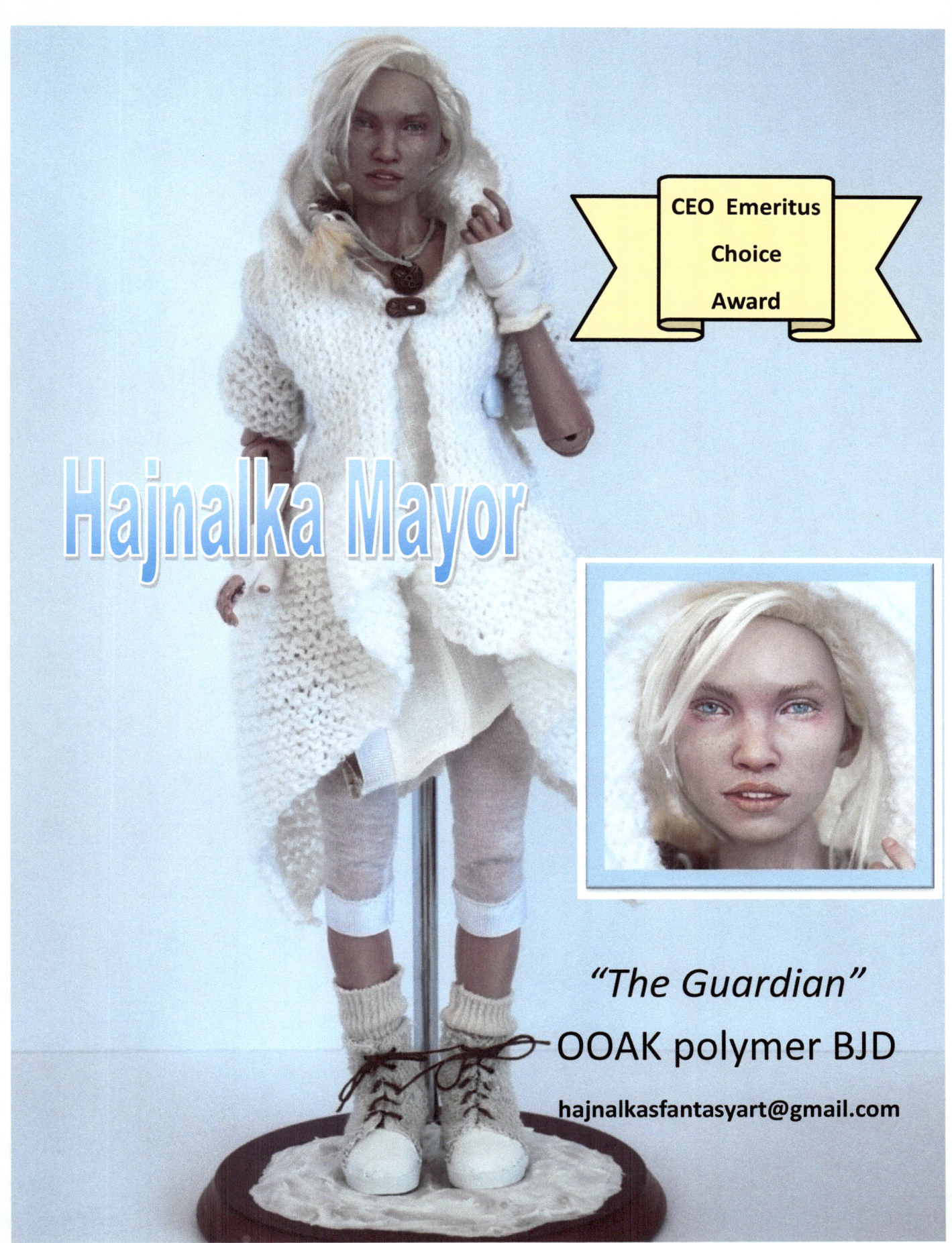

Hajnalka Mayor

CEO Emeritus Choice Award

"The Guardian"
OOAK polymer BJD
hajnalkasfantasyart@gmail.com

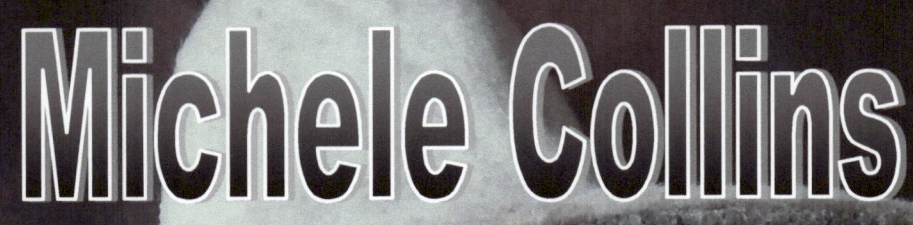

Michele Collins

Artists Choice Award

"Gandalf"

collinstoyemporium@yahoo.com

Raphael Nuri

"Graceful BJD"

rafaelbjd@yahoo.com

Best of Show Award

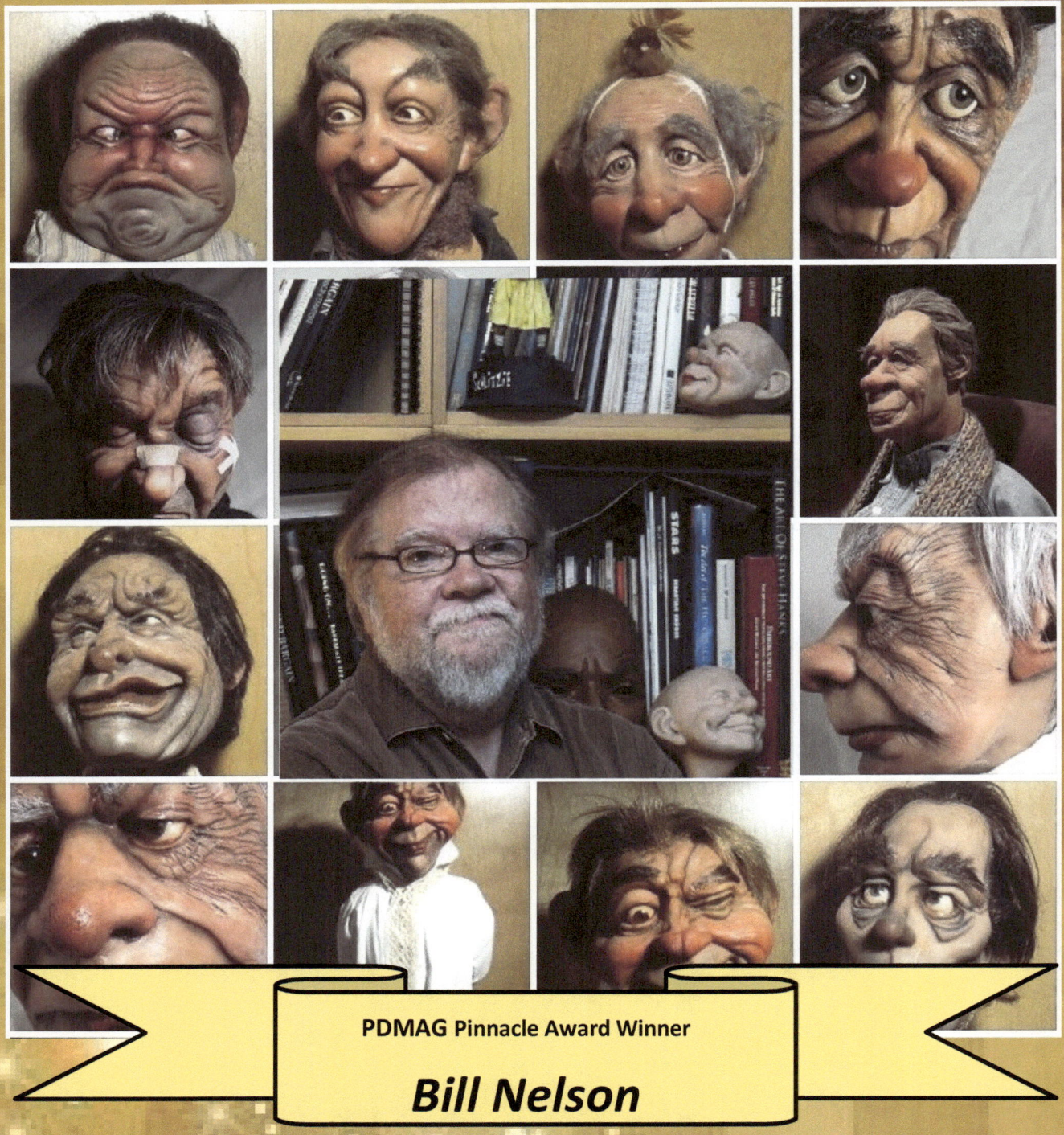

PDMAG Pinnacle Award Winner
Bill Nelson

This award is given as recognition the very best in the industry. The artists who receive this award were chosen because of their dedication to the excellence, innovation, and originality in the practice of doll making that is world renowned. What makes an artist a good choice for our Pinnacle award is the artist reached back to those coming up behind them and took it upon themselves to teach these new artists via tutorials, web instruction and live classes. They also have demonstrated a high level of dedication to the doll industry and a notably strong commitment to the ooak art doll community by promoting and advertising not just themselves but their peers. They bring their impressive talents to the forefront and inspire the next generation of artists which is how the industry grows. We are honored to be able to present these awards to these amazing talented and giving artists.

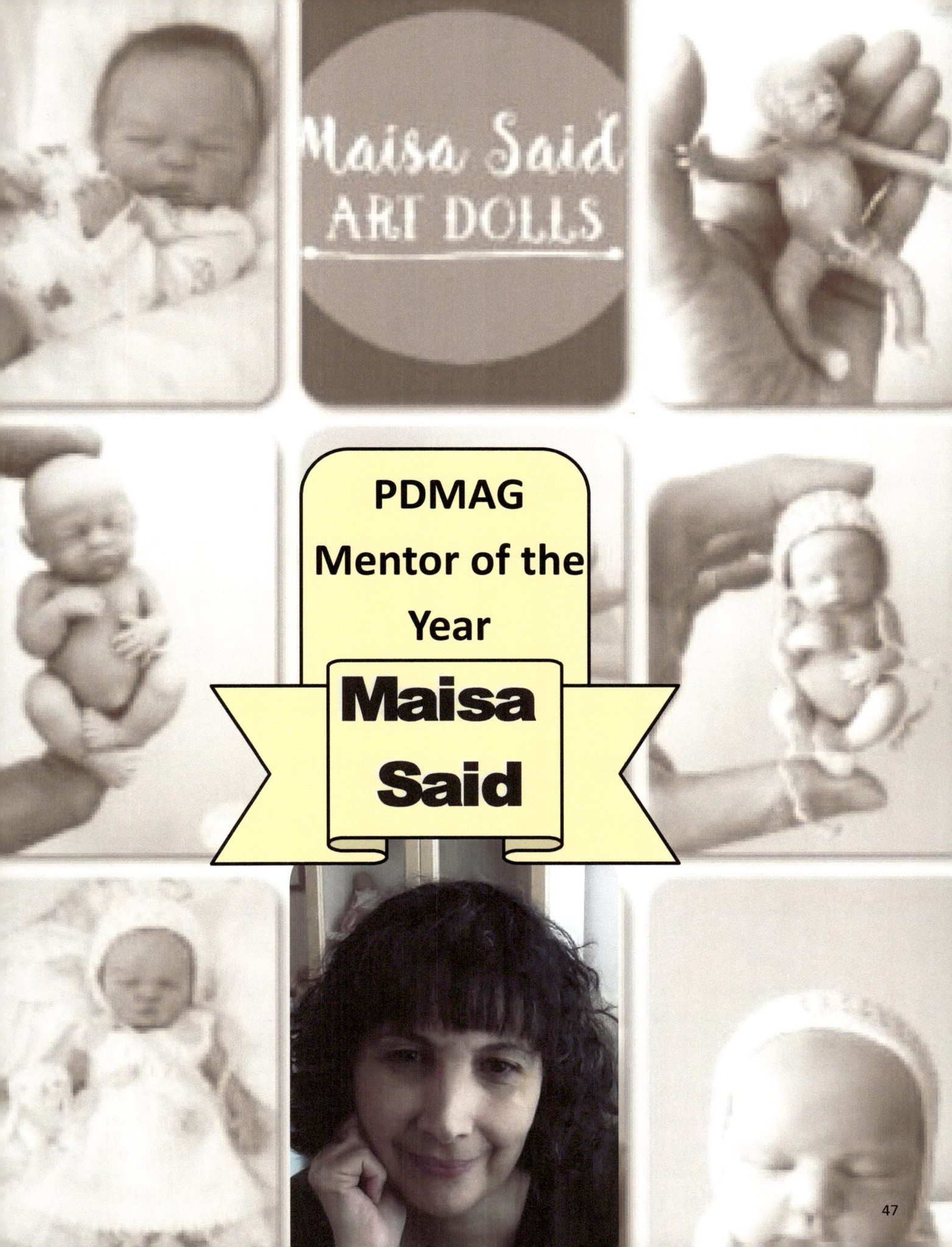

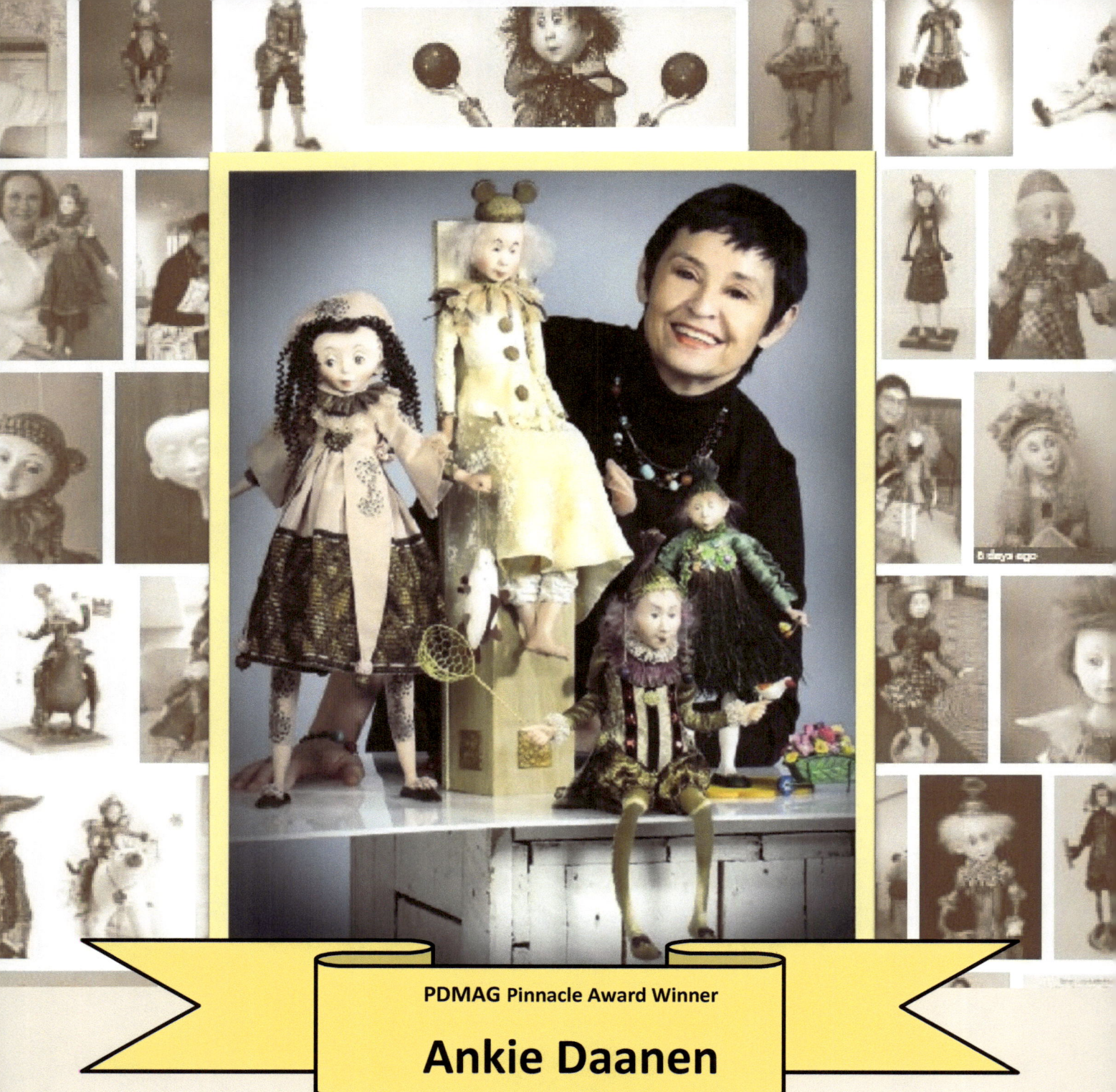

PDMAG Pinnacle Award Winner
Ankie Daanen

This award is given as recognition the very best in the industry. The artists who receive this award were chosen because of their dedication to the excellence, innovation, and originality in the practice of doll making that is world renowned. What makes an artist a good choice for our Pinnacle award is the artist reached back to those coming up behind them and took it upon themselves to teach these new artists via tutorials, web instruction and live classes. They also have demonstrated a high level of dedication to the doll industry and a notably strong commitment to the ooak art doll community by promoting and advertising not just themselves but their peers. They bring their impressive talents to the forefront and inspire the next generation of artists which is how the industry grows. We are honored to be able to present these awards to these amazing talented and giving artists.

A look inside Panenek Museum of Czech Republic by Vikki Ebbeling

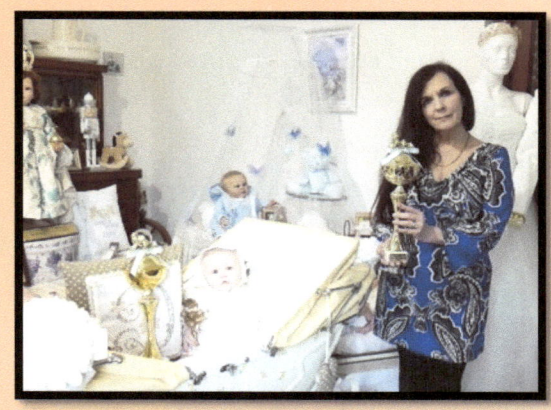

Freedom of Expression... is one of the most sought after things in LIFE. Imagine being able to put our utmost expressions into an Art Form that reveals our deepest thoughts and feelings. When this is accomplished the true unleashing of the expression of "soul" enters the Universe for all to view. Being born in the likeness of our universal creator... we all have the potential and ability to create beauty!!!

What gives us the desire to create? What is it that drives us forward with these vivid visions? A steady walk.. at times a jog or full blown run... to finish just what we've begun. It becomes our passion ... an obsession. There is a deep satisfaction when our creations reach the finish line. It is a gentle releasing of our hearts goal. We look at it ... and at times we wonder who created such a marvelous piece of work. We look at it and see into our own souls. We realize the true beauty of who we are.... in the reflections of our own art. We embrace it... because it is a part of ourselves. In some it is hidden deep within ... only to be unearthed and found. Like finding a diamond in the rough... there it will be.... Just waiting to be discovered within!!! All that is needed... is the willingness to tap into it!! If it is polymer clay that we choose as our medium of expression we need to take that piece of polymer clay in our hands ... feel it... warm it... make it become a part of us ... and we a part of it!!! We must allow ourselves to push it and shape it with our fingers....form it without thinking about what we will make. Let the clay speak to our hearts. Let it unfold. Then we will begin to see that it will work with us. These are the roots to our inner selves. The part of us that is one with nature.

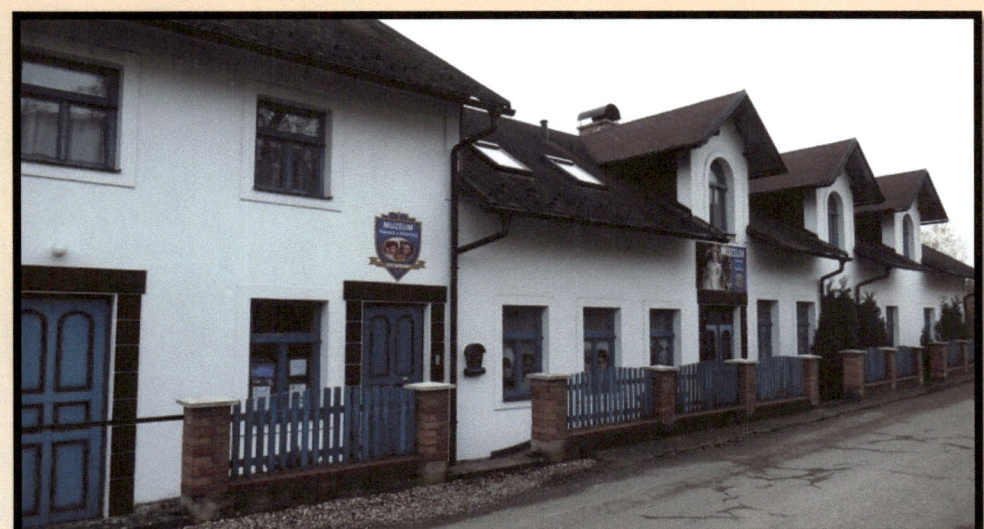

the part of us that is Soul. It is said that an artist bears their heart and soul into their creation. This is where it all begins. This is when a true artist is born... and the creation from within is born. We all have this ability to create in some way... it can come to us in any medium of choice....to portray anything we wish. It all comes from the desire in our hearts. We are looking at the potential to be anything we want to be.

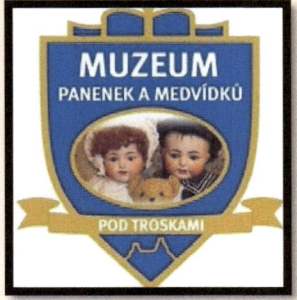

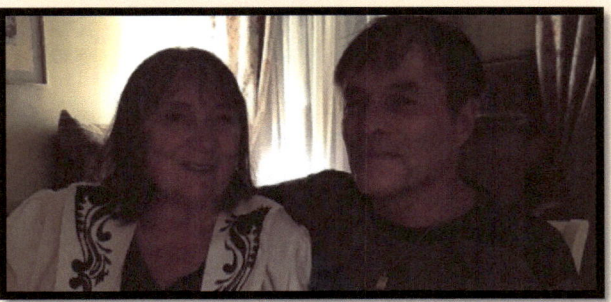

This Museum of Dolls and Teddy-bears... is directed by the Lovely Lady 'Nad'a Simkova.

Art Museums are a wonderful way to preserve the Art works of old and new expressions.

There is such a museum in the Czech Republic called: "Panenek Museum of Czech Republic"!!!!

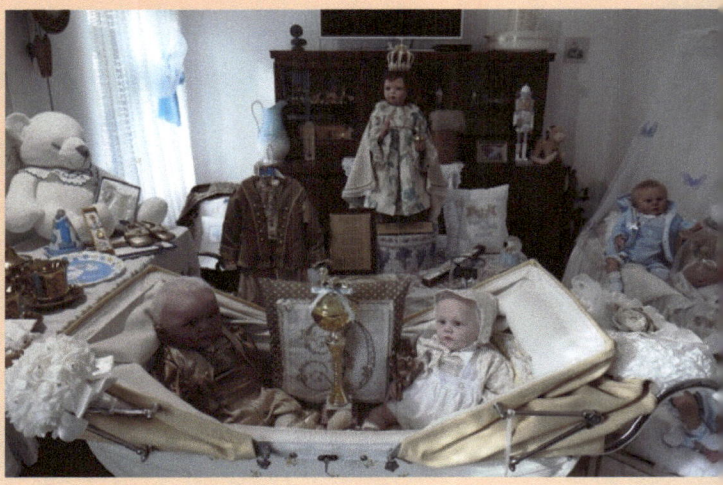

This Museum of Dolls and Teddy-bears... is directed by the Lovely Lady 'Nad'a Simkova. There is SO much Soul captured in this one very special museum. It is breathtaking... and it is blessed with many extremely high quality ART pieces from Artists all over the world. In this one single place the huge collection of various art forms include "One Of A Kind" figurative dolls... fantasy figurines such as mermaids, fairies, aliens, angels and Demons ... OOAK baby dolls ... preemie babies ... and animals of all kinds. Art created in ALL different mediums, including polymer clay, resin, cloth, composition, paper Mache', porcelain, celluloid, vinyl, silicone... are displayed with careful and deliberate consideration, to please the eyes of the observer....like "tasty sweet confections".

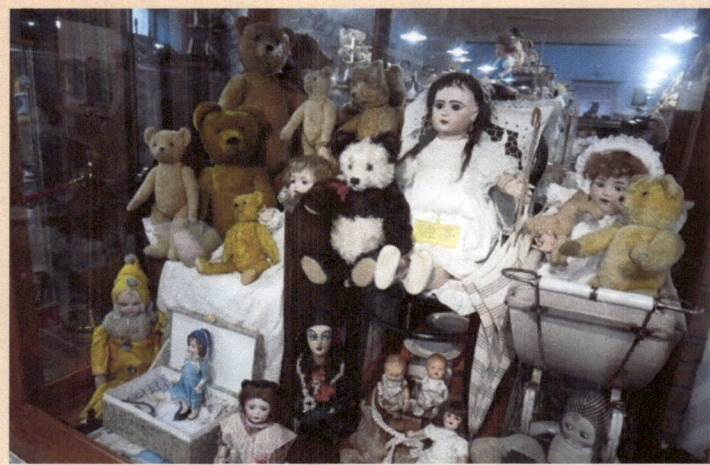

There are the most beautiful prams... cribs... cradles, day beds and hospital isolet's in arrangements with pram covers... pillows and assorted bed coverings created with so much beauty. They are made in silks, satin, brocades ......adorned with embroideries and hand-made roses, with imported new and old antique laces and trims. Exquisite baby clothing, displayed in beautiful array... in the loveliest of fabrics, laces and trims, all displayed as forms of art. Nad'a is truly gifted in arranging, organizing and bringing all things together in a very beautiful manner that complements each and every article in her displays. She also gives her honest opinion as a great Lover of the Art world herself . She quotes about her deep feelings and connection to the world of Art.

"Nad'a's quotes

My first life motto: "The doll was born to live in us. She gave joy, love, happiness, feeling that one is not alone. Love her and discover there is more than a memory of childhood. Get to know her and accept all, what she so generously offers. Together with us promote her more than only a mere child's toy " My greatest pleasure to exhibit artistic dolls of artists from the whole world.

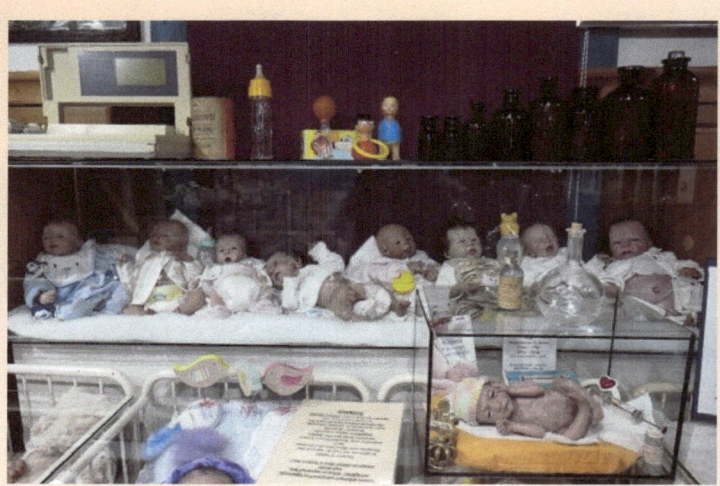

The artist and observer become one. The LOVE magically possessed by the piece of art has the purpose of conveying ones thoughts. Reality and fantasy have become one and the same. ART is a beautiful way to speak our hearts universally. Perhaps spoken Language originated from a lack of artistic expression. Imagine our original Art Work ... to be in a "timeless place of preservation" ...uniquely displayed for many observers and lovers of Art ...all around the world to enjoy.

I would like every lover and collector of dolls to realize that at the beginning of the birth of each doll is always a sculptor. Today so popular reborn dolls, silicone and porcelain dolls would never arise without the hard work of the sculptor. For this reason I consider the modeled unique – OOAK dolls as the true collector's jewel of our exhibition for our museum. Many of our exhibited dolls have won the highest awards in world competitions. It is a great honor for us that the artists have entrusted their winning dolls or their best art work to our hands. The art dolls bring enjoyment for the eyes of lovers of dolls from all over the world.

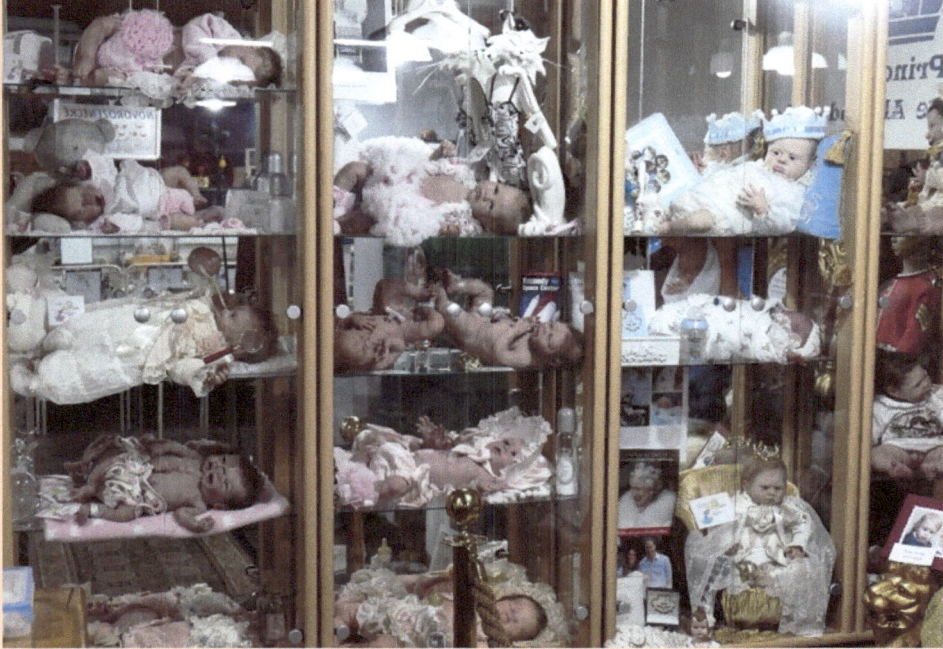

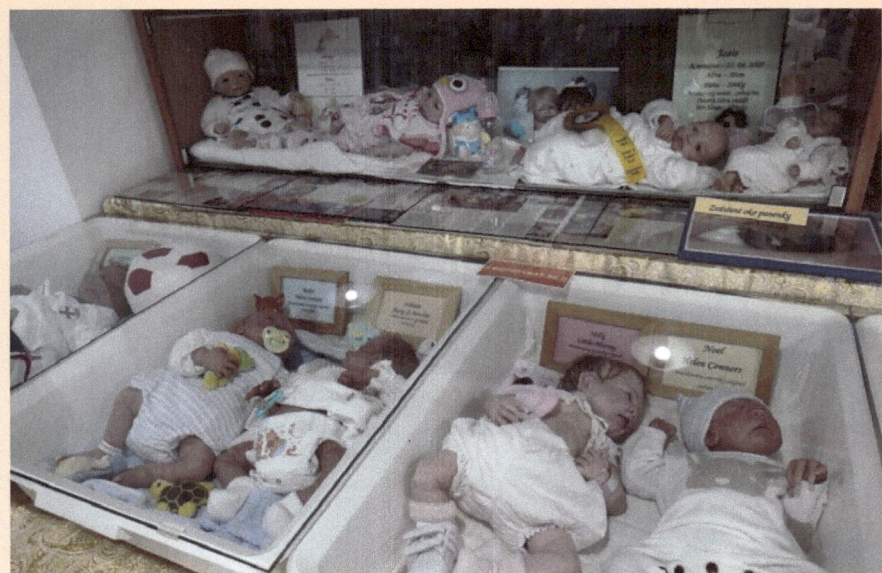

It is wonderful that there are currently so many talented sculptors of dolls. It is very important for the older generations to pass on their experiences to the younger generation. Only in this way will the "phenomenon art doll" be maintained.

Our museum is trying hard to show the whole historical development of dolls. The new art doll is an integral part of this development. We believe that the magic works of sculptors will be will be maintained for all future generations.

My second life motto:

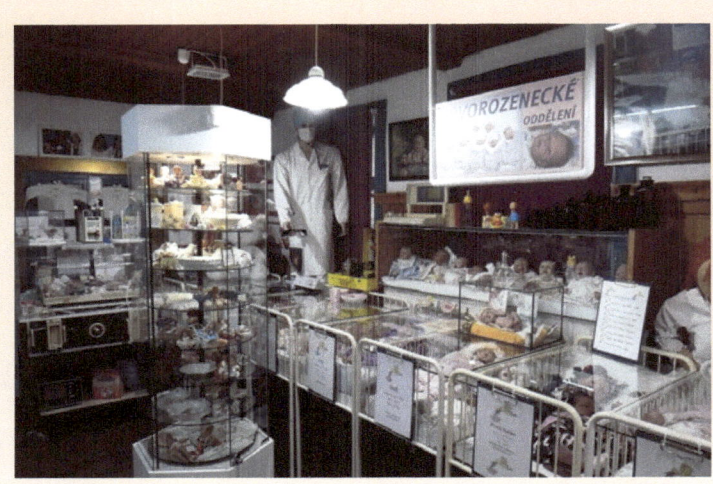

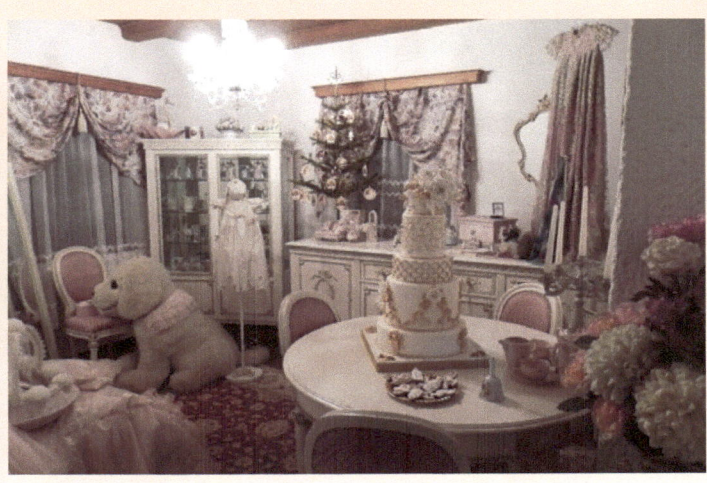

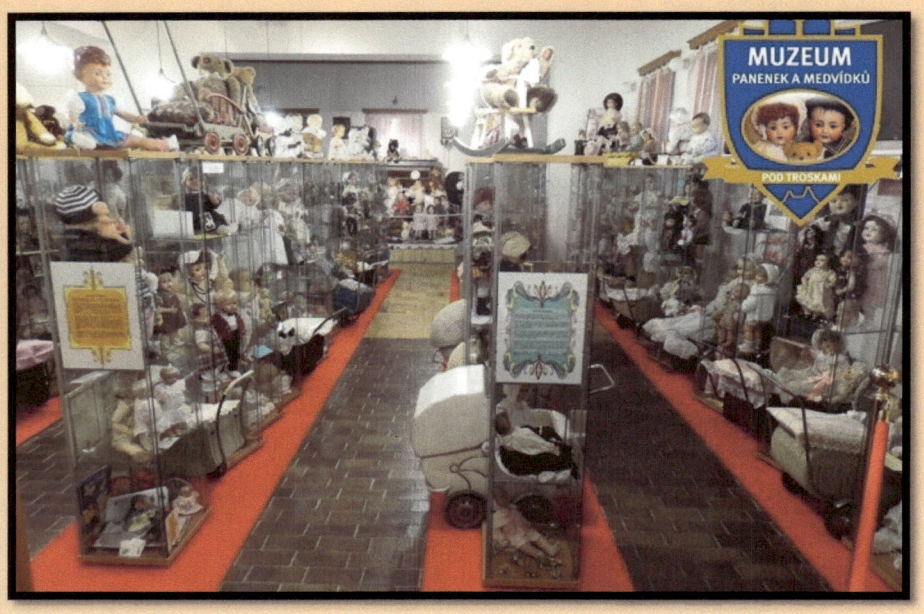

"The world of dolls is a world of dreams and to live in dreams is a dream "

End of Quote:

Nad'a is always scouting for new pieces of art to add to her already magnificent displays within the museum.

She likes to contact the artist herself when a piece catches her eye ... or speaks to her soul.

Nad'a searches for original "One of a kind" art... sculpted, created and mostly completed by the original Artist. The joy of creating an art piece and having it displayed and preserved in such a beautiful museum is a true honor. If anyone ever has the chance to travel to this magnificent museum ... you will have the experience of a lifetime.

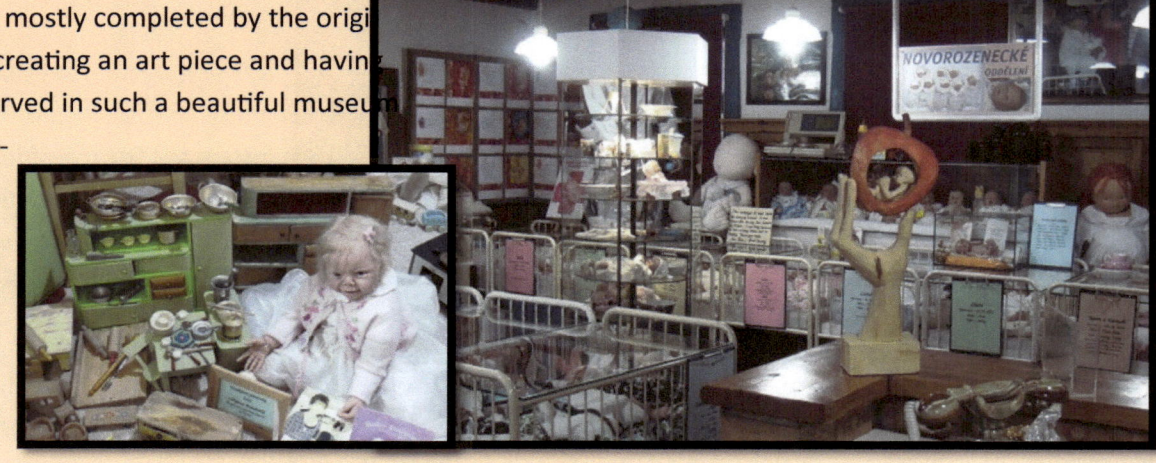

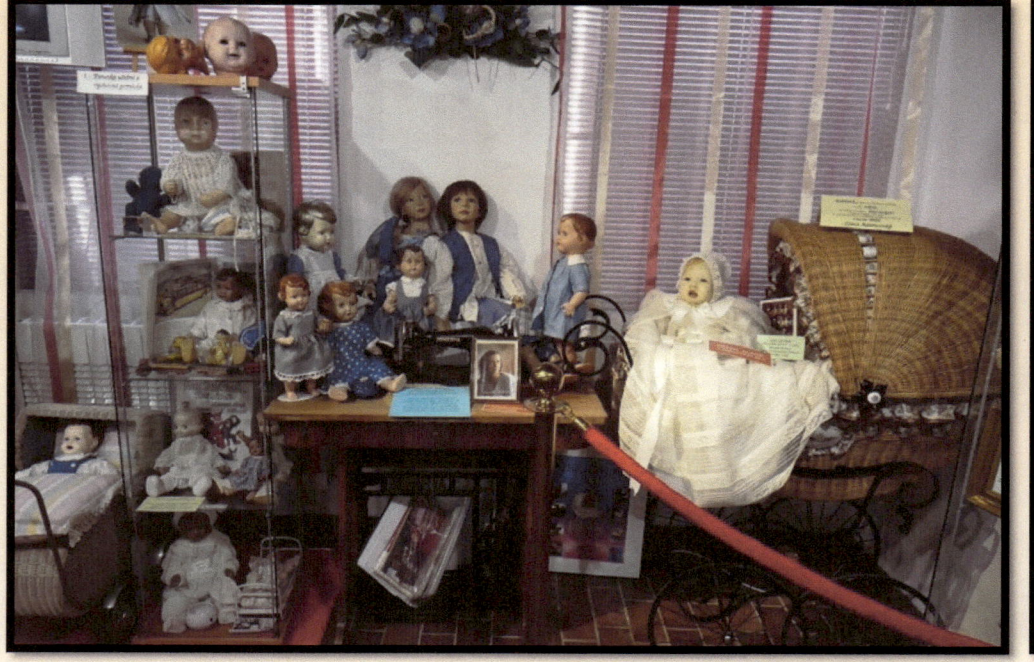

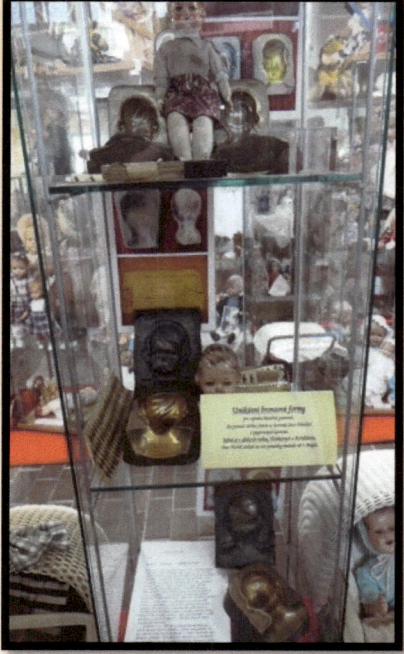

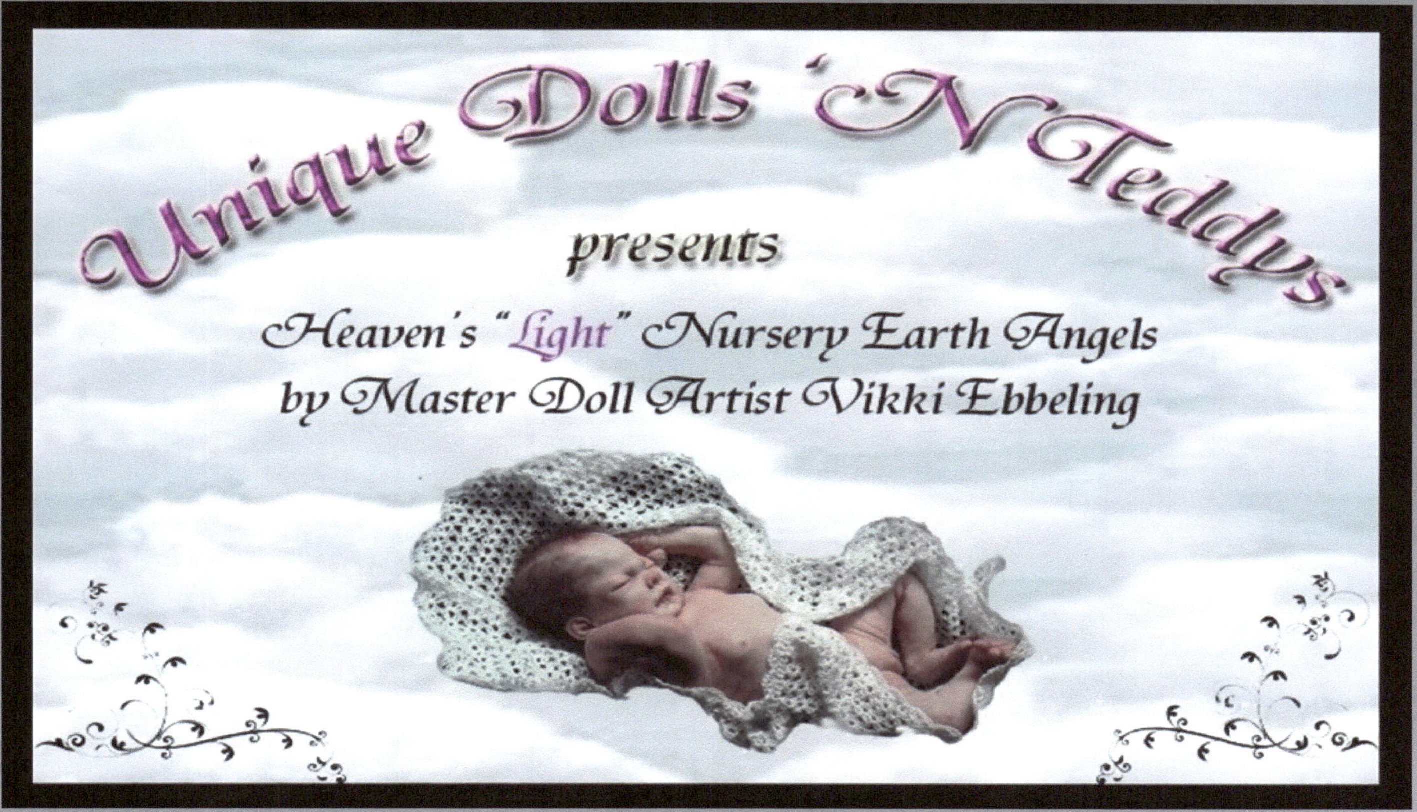

Unique Dolls 'N Teddys

presents

Heaven's "Light" Nursery Earth Angels
by Master Doll Artist Vikki Ebbeling

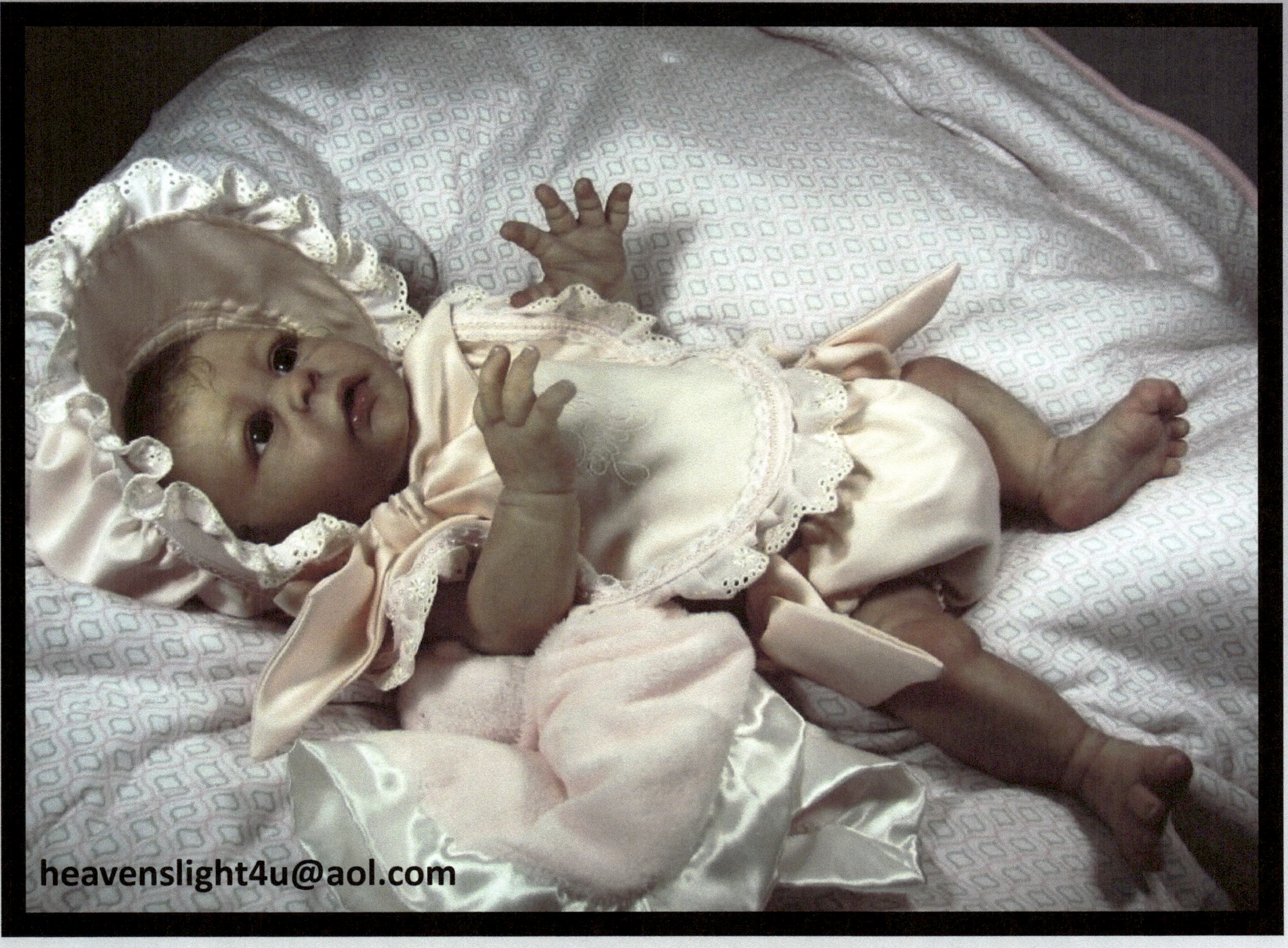

heavenslight4u@aol.com

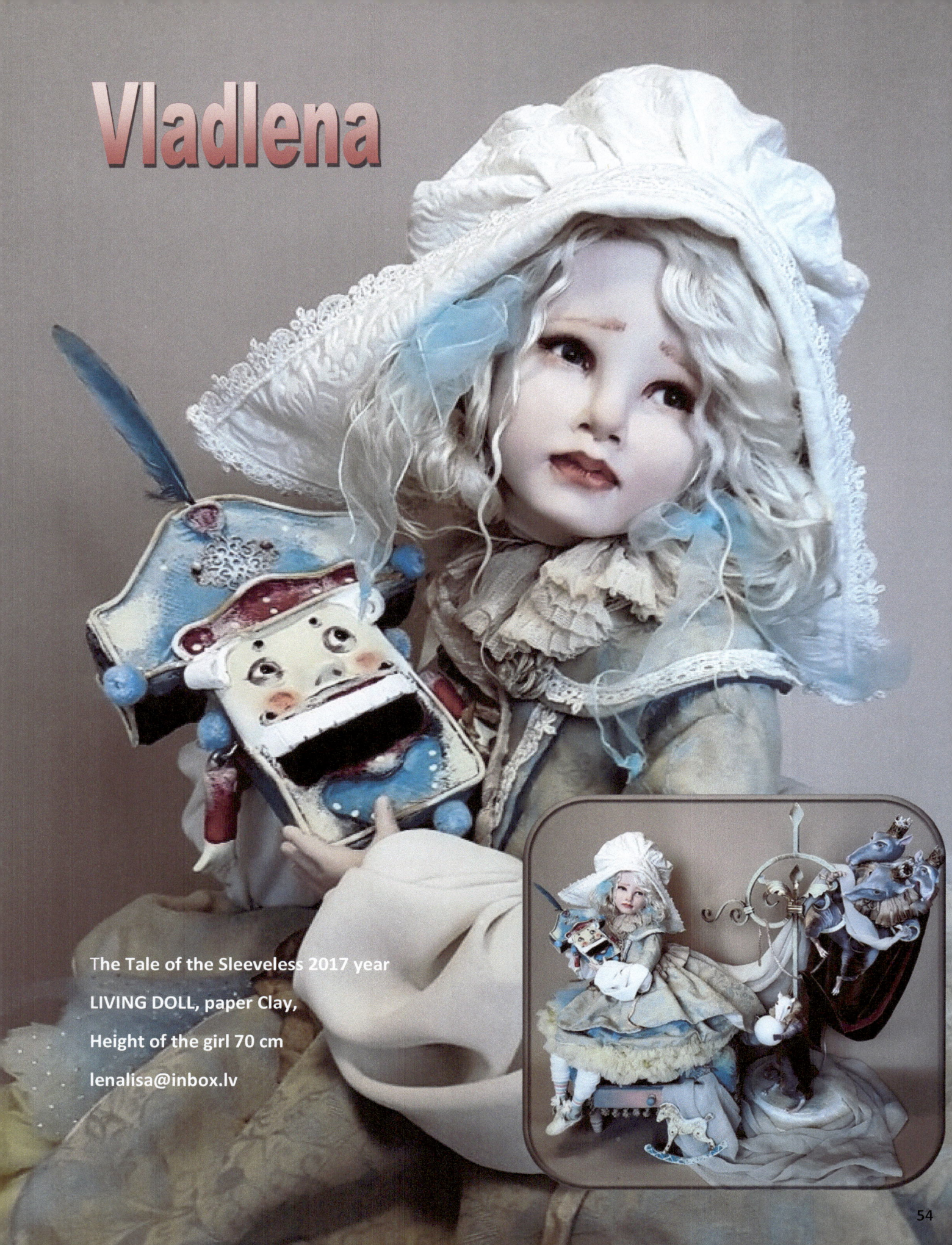

Vladlena

The Tale of the Sleeveless 2017 year
LIVING DOLL, paper Clay,
Height of the girl 70 cm
lenalisa@inbox.lv

Loredana Salvo

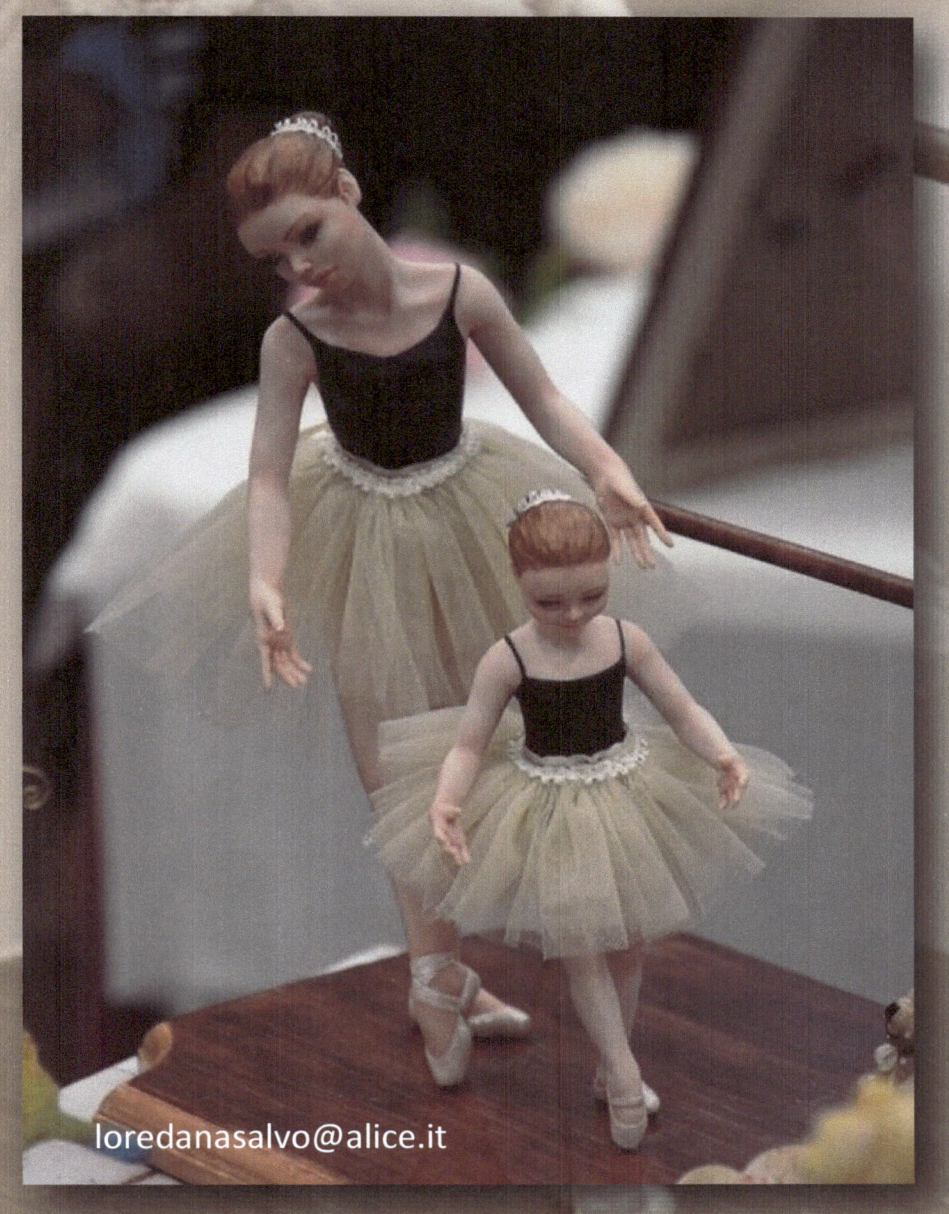

Good morning

I would like to introduce myself and introduce you to "Le gioie diLulu"

I love art in all its forms. I studied sculpture, wood carving, painting, ceramic decoration and even tailoring and fashion modeling.

I have worked in almost all these areas, especially the ceramic decoration that has occupied an important part of my life.

Three years ago I met the world of polymer clay that changed my world. I returned to my first true love "sculpture".

Now I create OOAK (one of a kind) on a 1: 6 scale. I like portraying women, but also fantasy figures such as fairies or mermaids, not even disregarding portraits.

Loredana

loredanasalvo@alice.it

Loredana Salvo

I love this kind of creation because it allows me to exploit all the skills I have acquired over the years and at the same time to experiment with new materials and techniques.

Every job is the result of a search to obtain more and more a result faithful to reality. Recently I created a sculpture inspired by "The Birth of Venus" by Sandro Botticelli, a work that I love and that I have been able to see several times in person since I am fortunate to live a few kilometers from the beautiful Florence, Italy.

Not much more than thirty centimeters high, everything has been modeled by me without the use of molds of any kind (even for the shell on which it rests) then laid on a rectangle of sea created with resin.

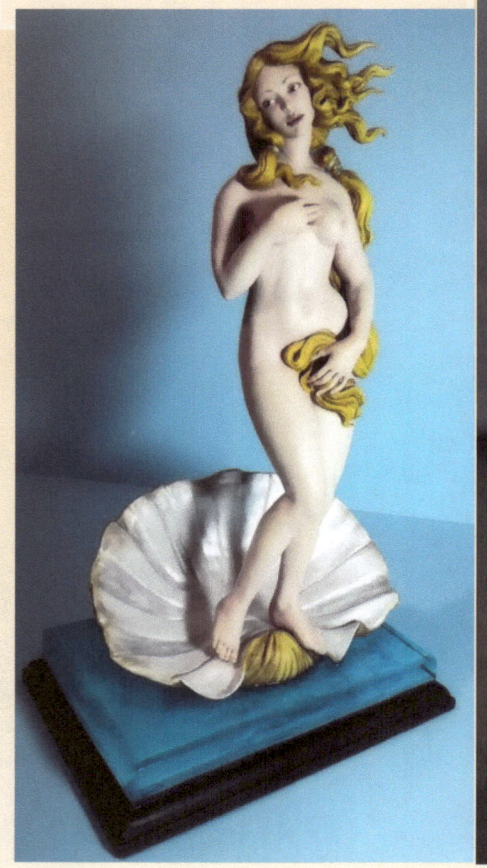

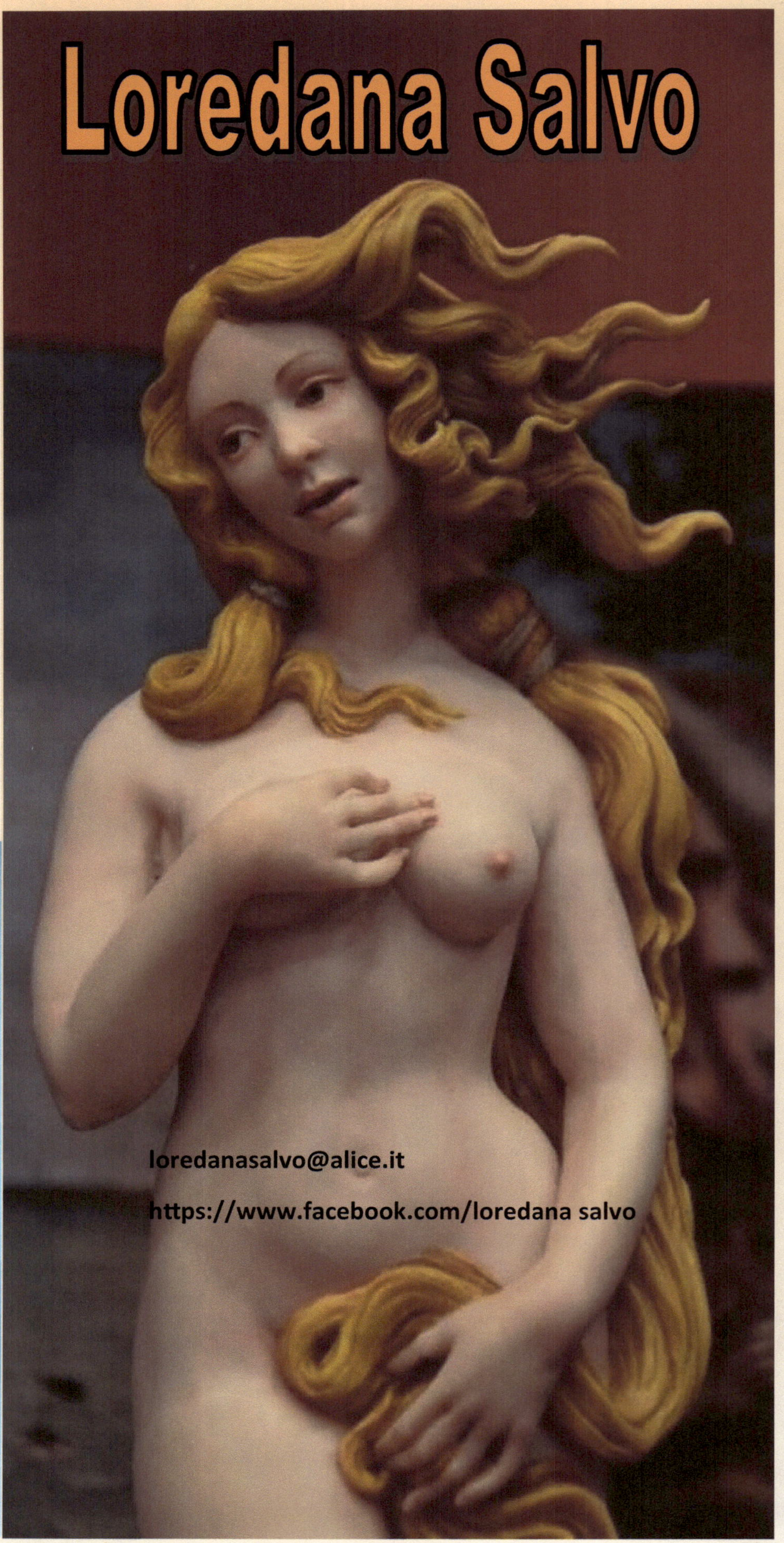

loredanasalvo@alice.it

https://www.facebook.com/loredana salvo

Karina Sewera

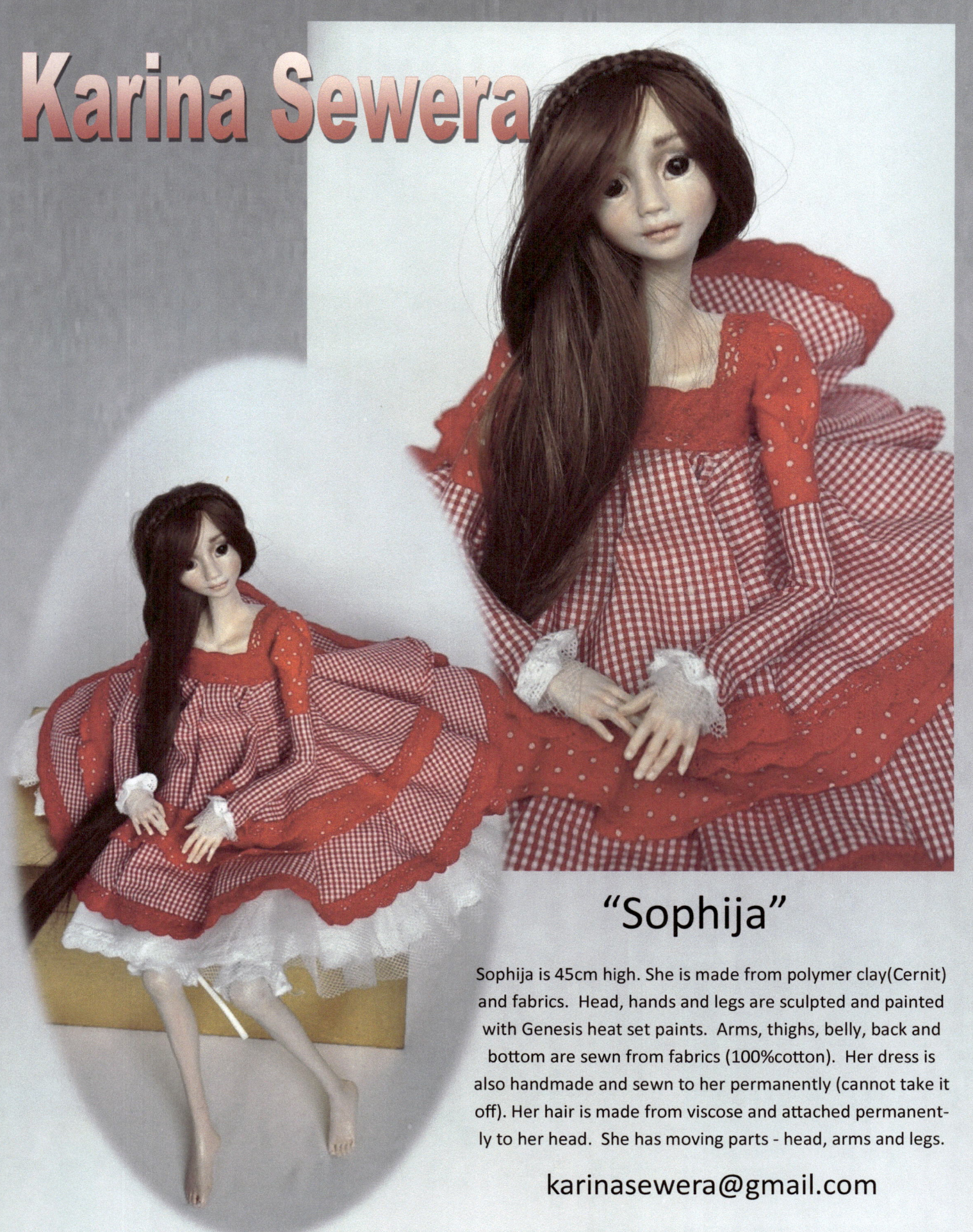

"Sophija"

Sophija is 45cm high. She is made from polymer clay(Cernit) and fabrics. Head, hands and legs are sculpted and painted with Genesis heat set paints. Arms, thighs, belly, back and bottom are sewn from fabrics (100%cotton). Her dress is also handmade and sewn to her permanently (cannot take it off). Her hair is made from viscose and attached permanently to her head. She has moving parts - head, arms and legs.

karinasewera@gmail.com

Anita Collins

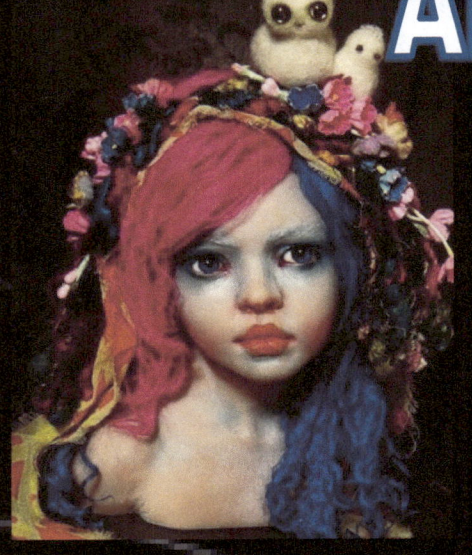
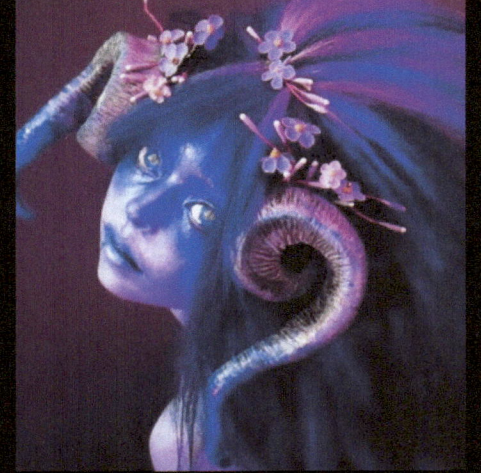
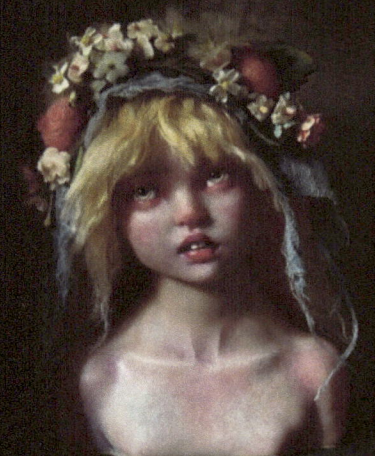
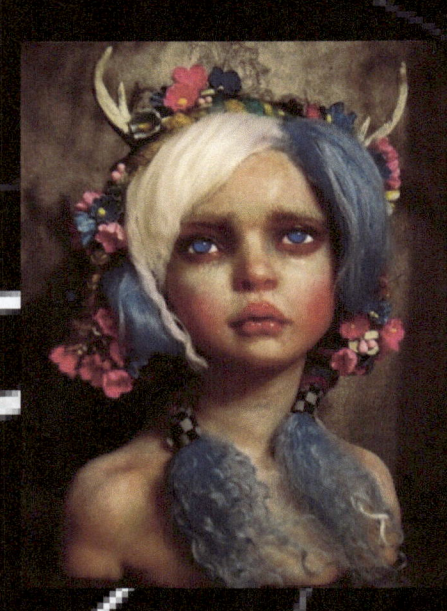
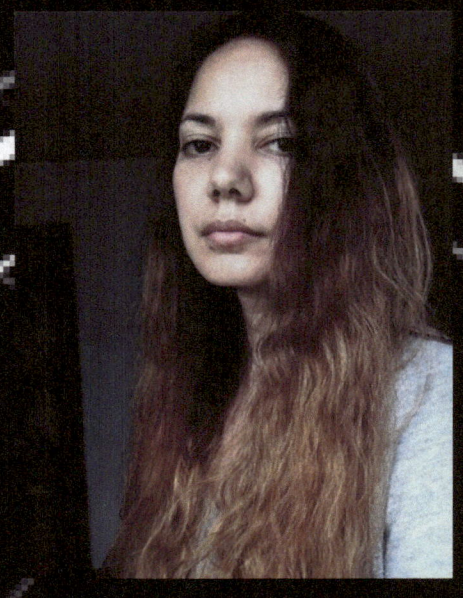
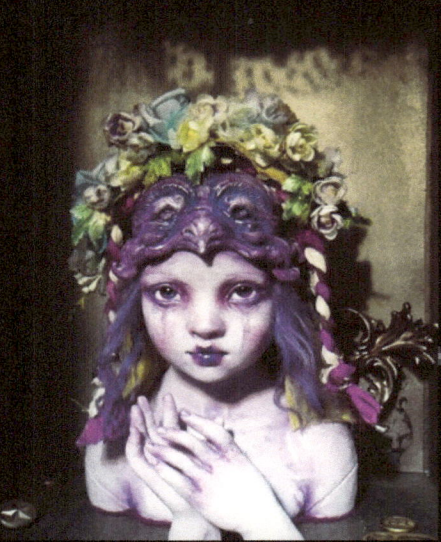
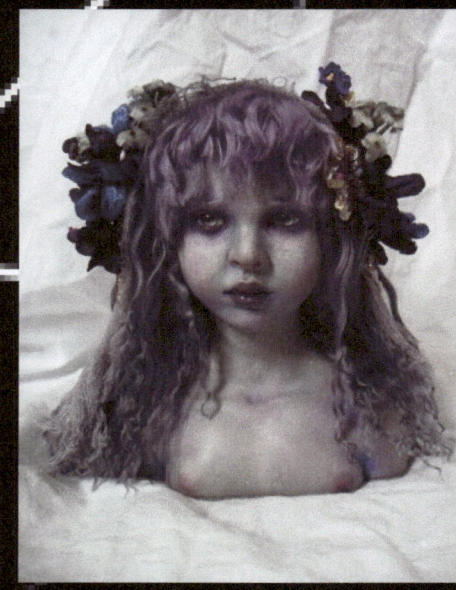
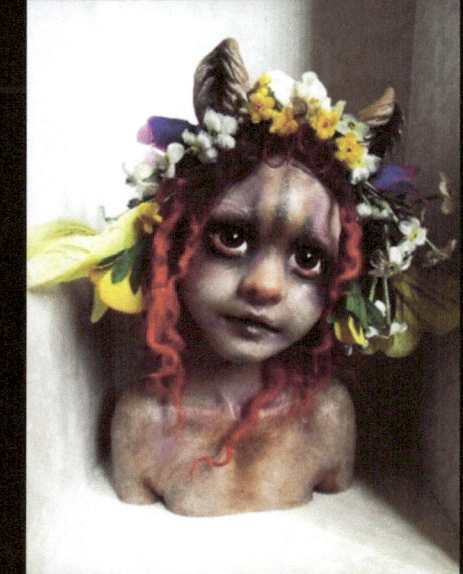
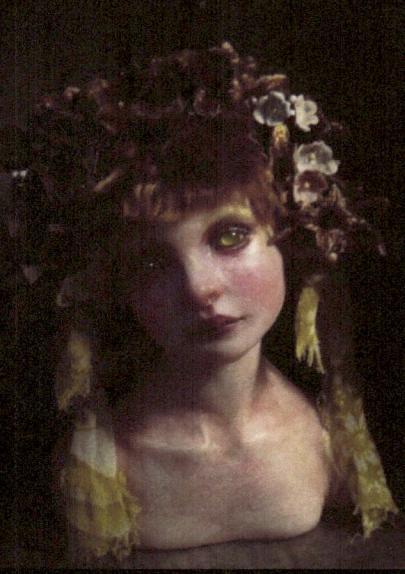

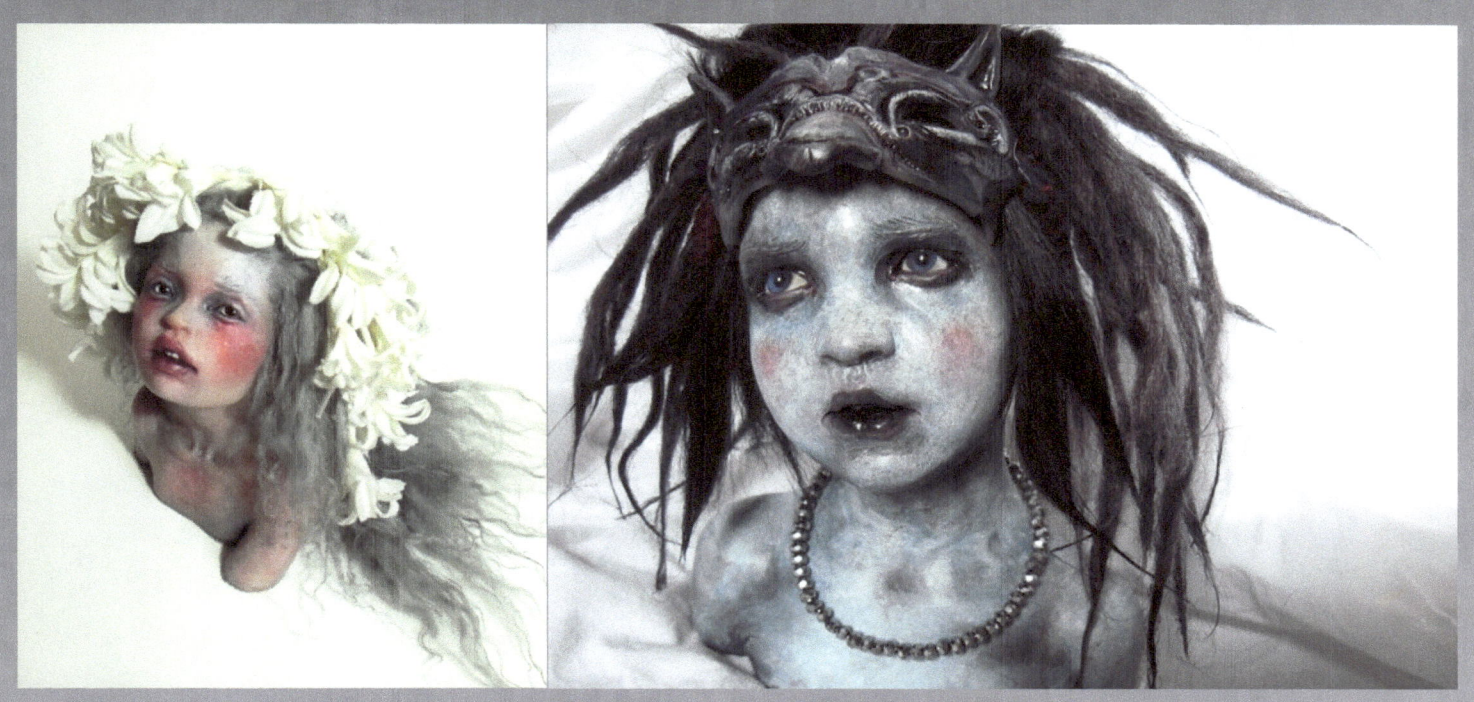

Anita Collins

sleetwealth@gmail.com

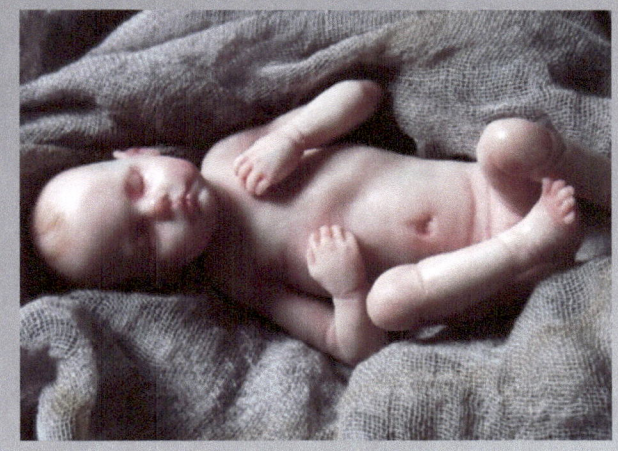

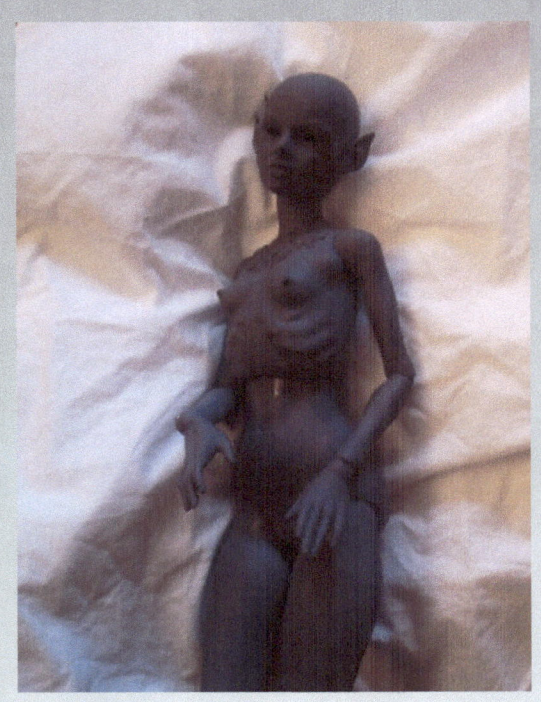

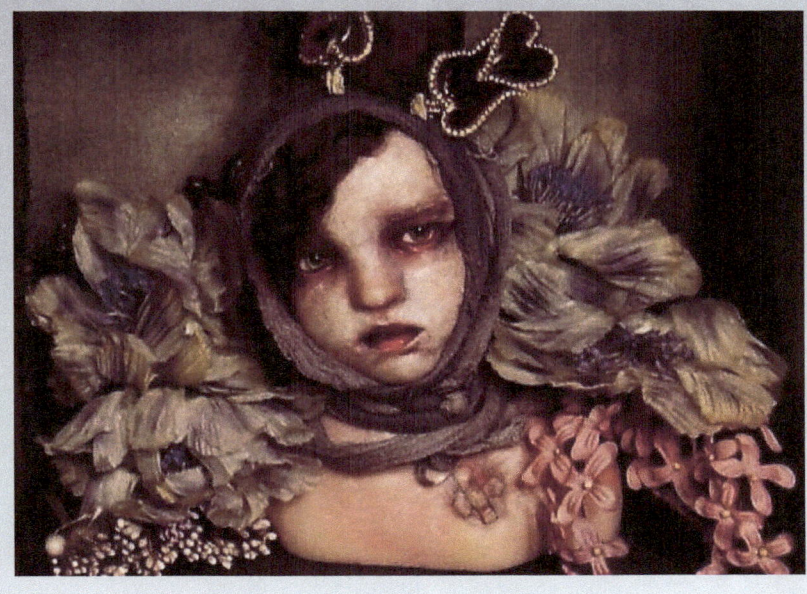

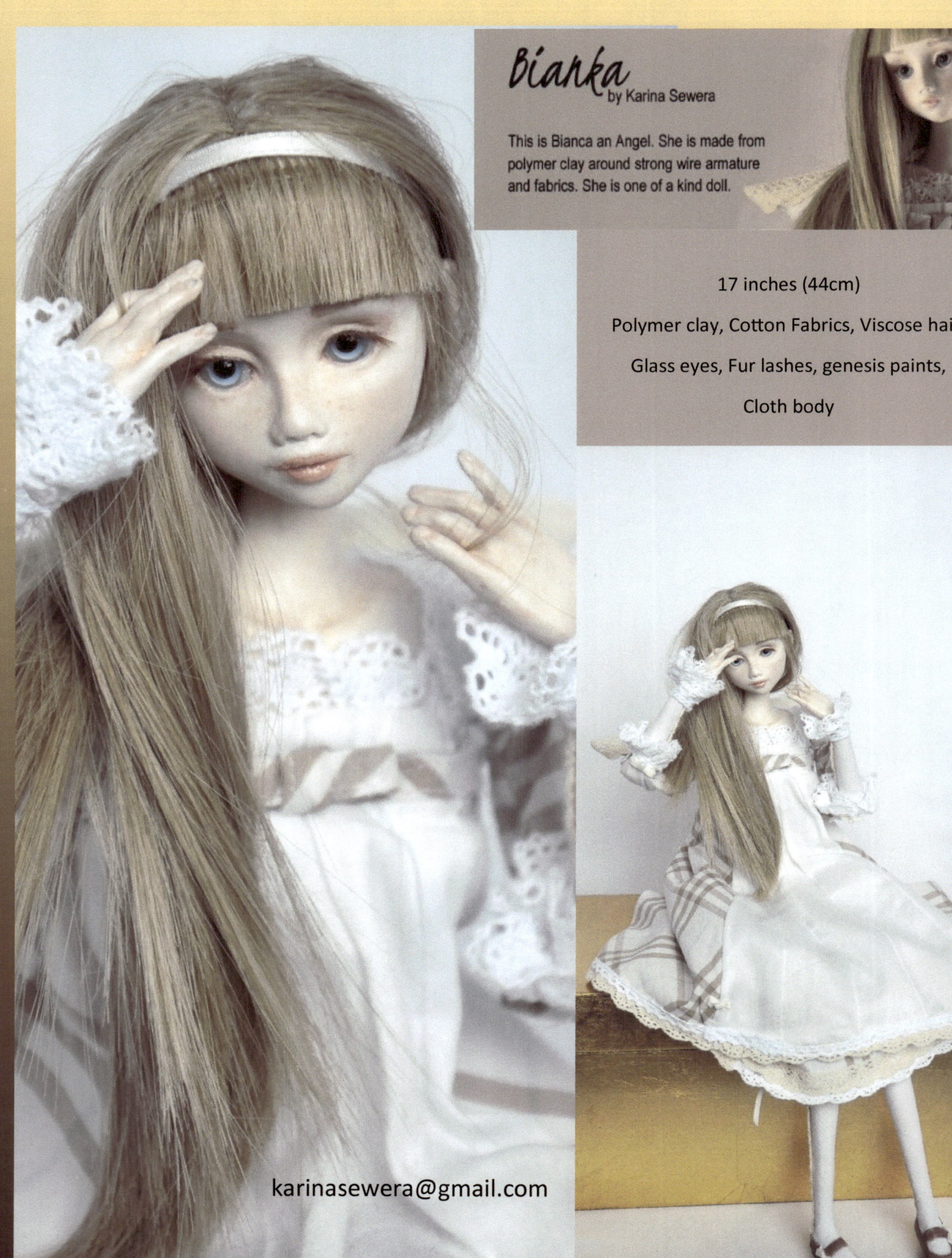

Shauna McCullough

"THE LAND OF MAKE BELIEVE"

Twenty-eight years ago, I became interested in the art of making dolls. The journey that led and inspired me to make one-of-a-kind dolls was rather interesting. My family owned a clothing store in Salt Lake City, Utah. I was in charge of window displays and thought it would be fun to incorporate a Santa or two at Christmas time to kind of spruce things up. I found some bland store bought Santa but I did not care for the look they gave my windows; the funny little dolls did not look quite right in such an elegant holiday window.

I decided to try my hand at making Santa dolls myself. It was frustrating. I couldn't figure out how to make the heads to stay on and how to have them not tip over. I didn't know what kind of clay to use, so I went to art supply store and bought some clay to make heads and hands for the dolls. I spent hours and hours on one doll. I thought you were suppose to bake this clay in the oven, but to my disappointment, I opened the oven door and found a pile of clay sitting on the cookie sheet (literally a pile of clay).

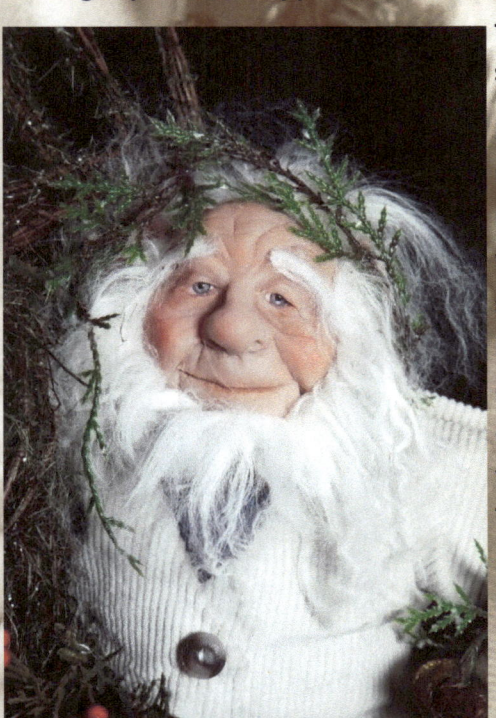

During the same holiday season, our local newspaper ran an article about a gentleman who was making the kind of dolls I wanted to make. The dolls were all hand-sculpted with a special clay and all had beautiful handmade clothing and were on display at a furniture store of all places. My mom and I immediately went there. What I saw there, changed my life. The dolls I saw was the work of a renowned master doll maker. My mother noticed classes were being offered so she bought one for me as a Christmas gift.

shaunadoll@gmail.com

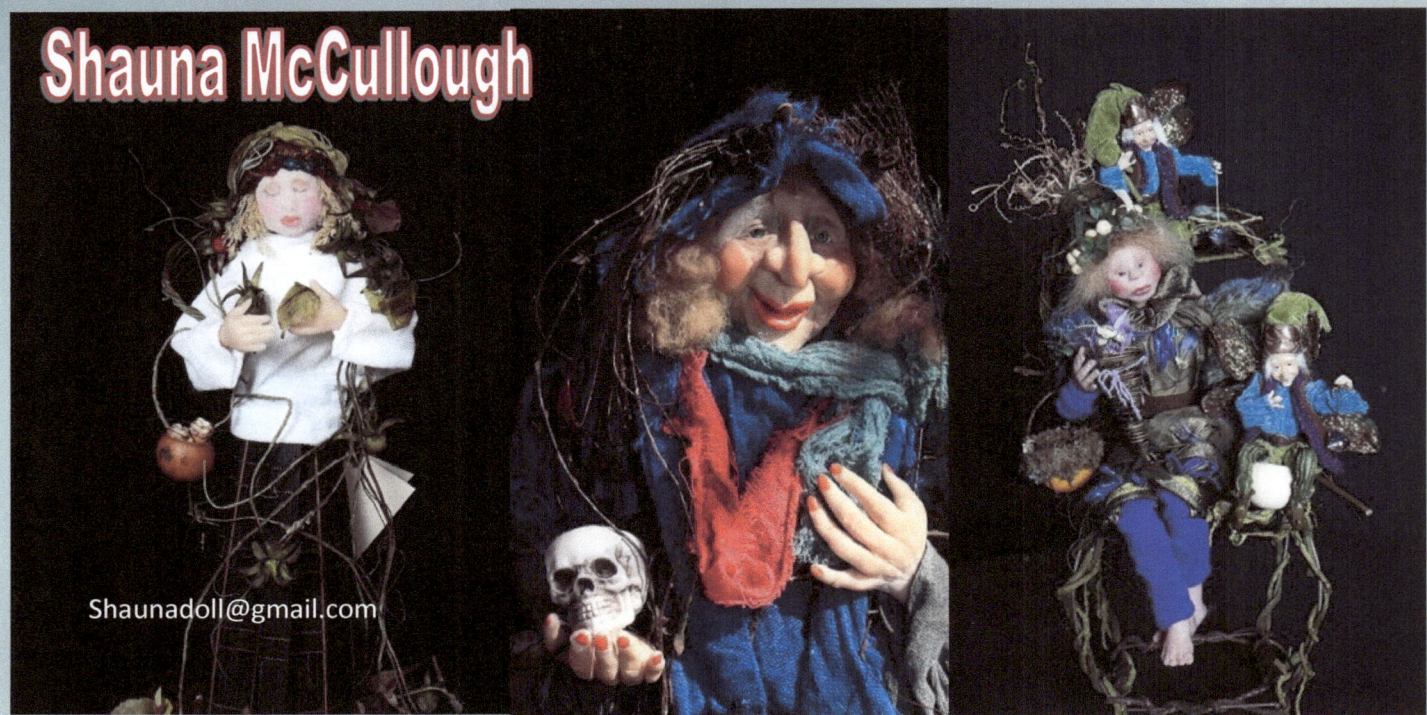

Shauna McCullough

Shaunadoll@gmail.com

My mother is now close to 97 years old still loves the dolls I learned to make and says it was the best gift she has ever given! She is still my inspiration and continues to support my love for doll making.

My window display became a form of art and as people would pass by they would stop and admire the art dolls and inquire if the dolls were for sale. Every evening after work, I would go home and work on new creations and all my dolls would sell. I am sure I spent more time and money on them than I actually made on them, but it didn't matter because my customers loved my dolls almost as much as I loved making them!

Fast forward 28 years, my custom studio is a landscape of heads, hands, and feet with boxes of plush wonderful textiles and accessories to fit any doll. I love making Santa but my desire to expand has opened a new world of many kinds of Art Dolls from Native American, African and of course my 'make-believe' Ethereal dolls.

Once the doll is complete they take on a life of their own and hopefully be a feast for the eyes and of the heart. I love the art of making dolls and may the journey continue for many years to come.

There is a segment of the population that for some reason thinks creating art dolls is a craft. The thought, the work, and the artistic skills that it takes to create these beautiful art dolls cannot be classified as crafts…….this is fine art! Check out the wonderful galleries where this 'fine art' is displayed and sold.

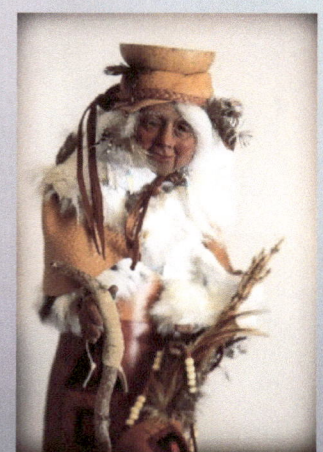
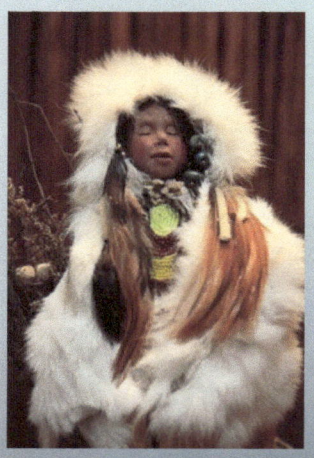
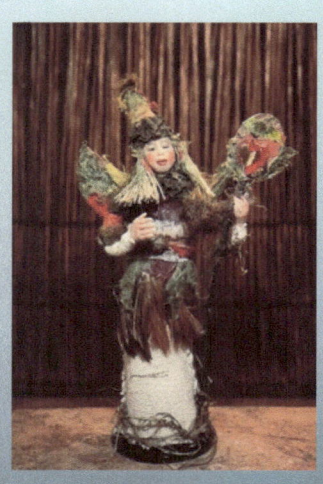

THE ANGEL DOLL COMPANY

- Learn to Sculpt
- Reborn Babies
- Doll Kits
- Paint A Friend
- Collectibles
- Silicone Doll Art
- OOAK Dolls
- Special Events
- Birthday Parties

45 N. Market St.
Lancaster, Pa 17603
717-947-4328
theangeldollcompany@gmail.com

Would you like to learn more about making an articulated cloth doll?

My new book "Making Angelina" is designed as a follow along work book. Each step is illustrated and designed for ease of use. It's a step-by-step guide filled with new techniques and useful hints that will help you create your own fully articulated Angelina doll and outfit!

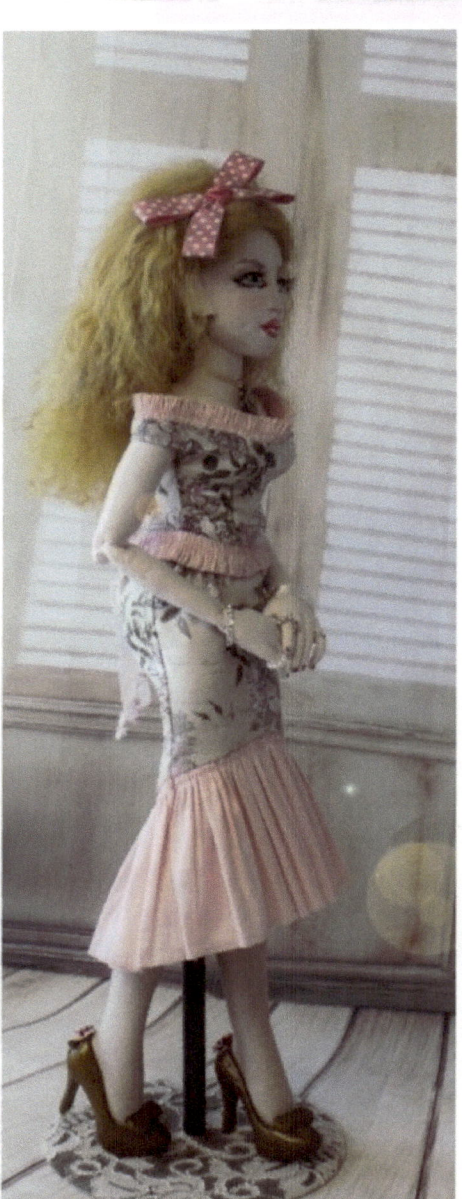

Angelina is a poseable, all-cloth art doll. Like the BJD (ball-jointed-doll) a CJD = (cloth-jointed-doll) is assembled from individually made parts, poseable, and of all cloth construction. She features 10 points of articulation: shoulders, elbows, wrists, hips and knees

Her measurements are:

- Height 21"
- Bust 8.5"
- Waist 6"
- Hips 10"
- Head 7"

She is an art doll, for adult collectors and not intended to be a child's toy.

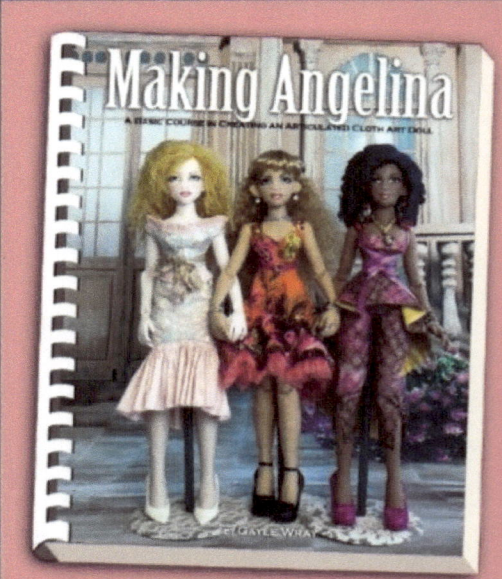

Available at http://gaylewraydolls.com
In person doll making classes available.

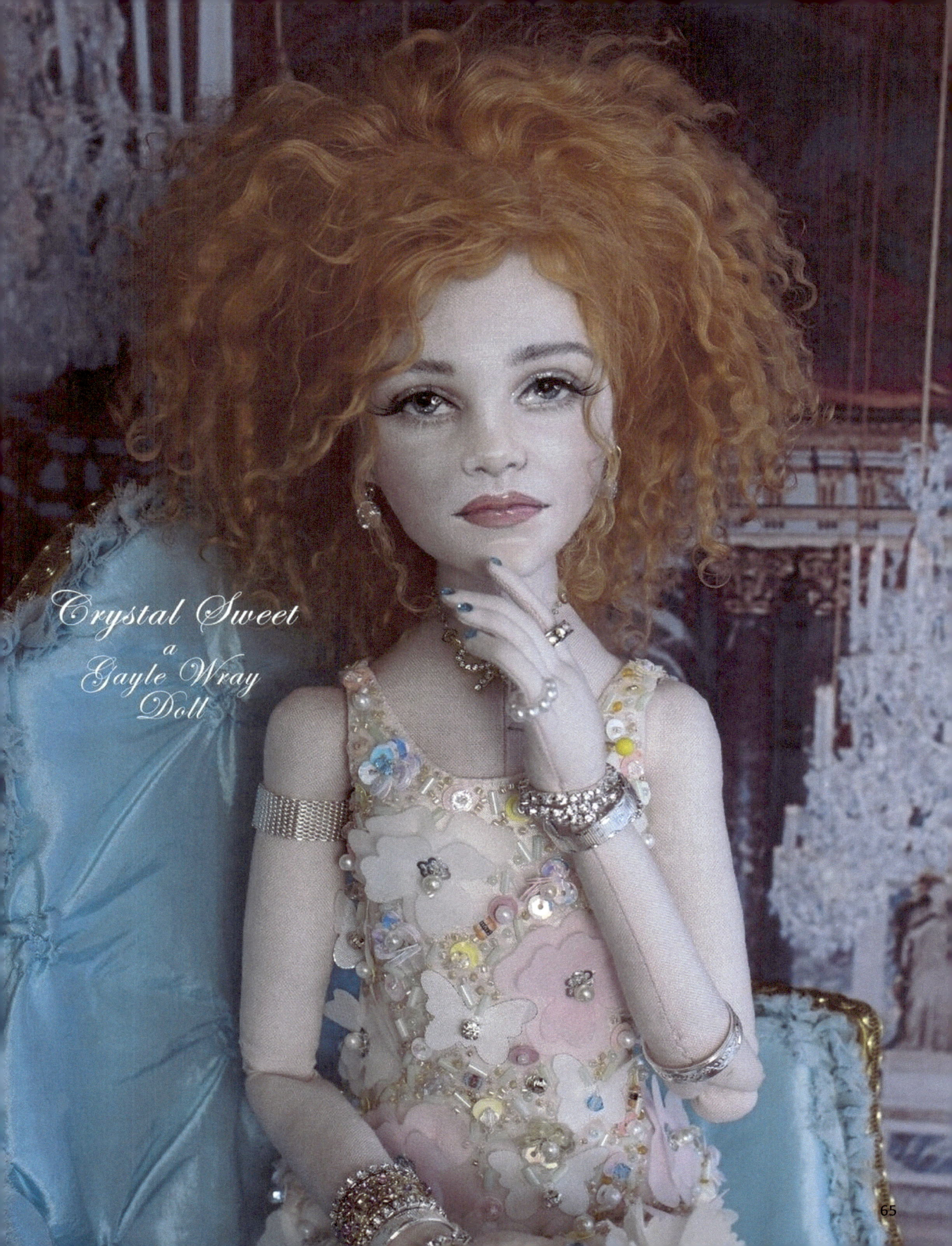
Crystal Sweet
a
*Gayle Wray
Doll*

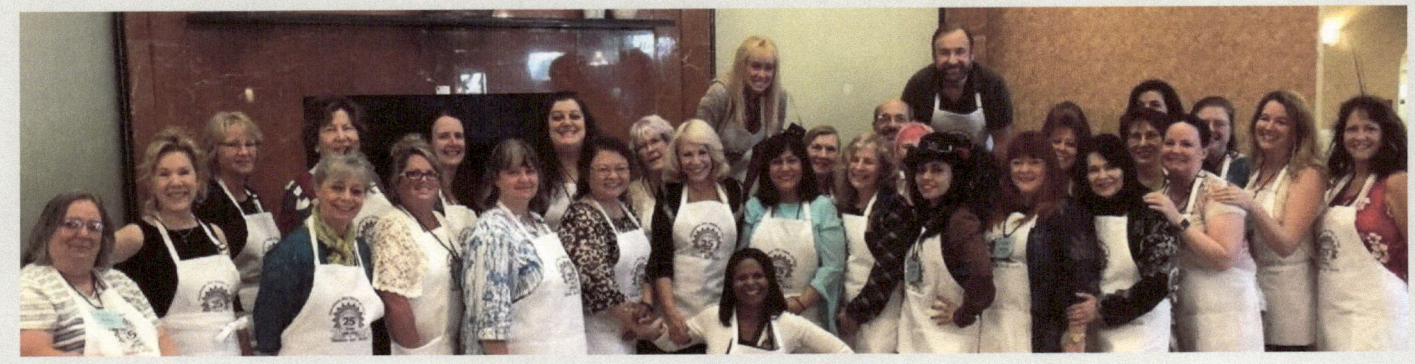

Join the Professional Doll Makers Art Guild

Whether your a Master doll artist who wants to share the experiences of doll making with kindred spirits or a new artist who wants guidance into this complex market or a complete beginner who would love to learn to make hand sculpted dolls and figurative sculptures of your own, PDMAG has a place for you.

Contact us at

Professionaldollmakers.com

to join our artists or enroll in the academy

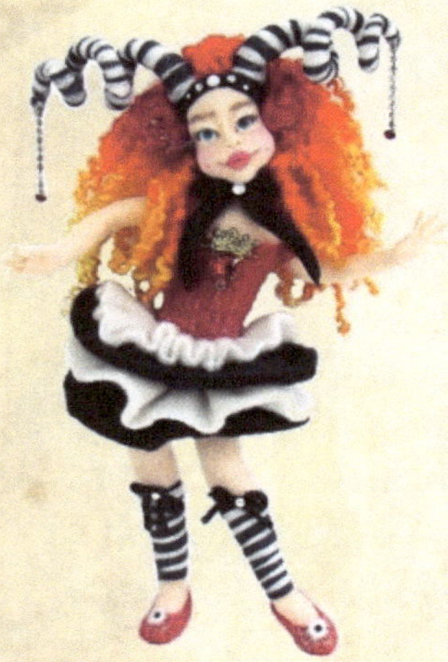

OooDolls

Handcrafted Needle Felt Dolls
Hand Dyed/Painted Doll Hair

Doll Artist: Colleen Spies

www.ooodolls.etsy.com
www.facebook.com/ooodolls

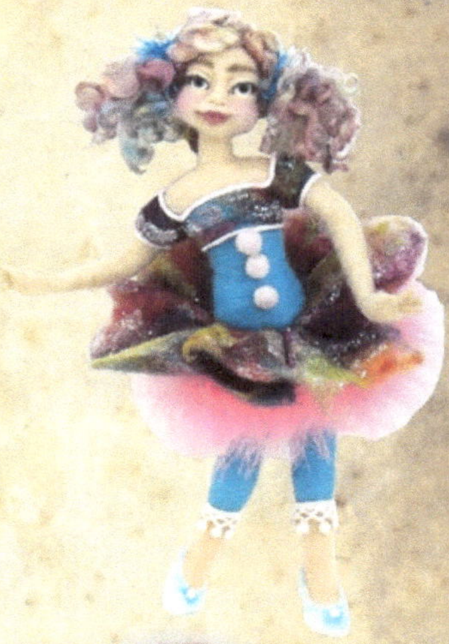

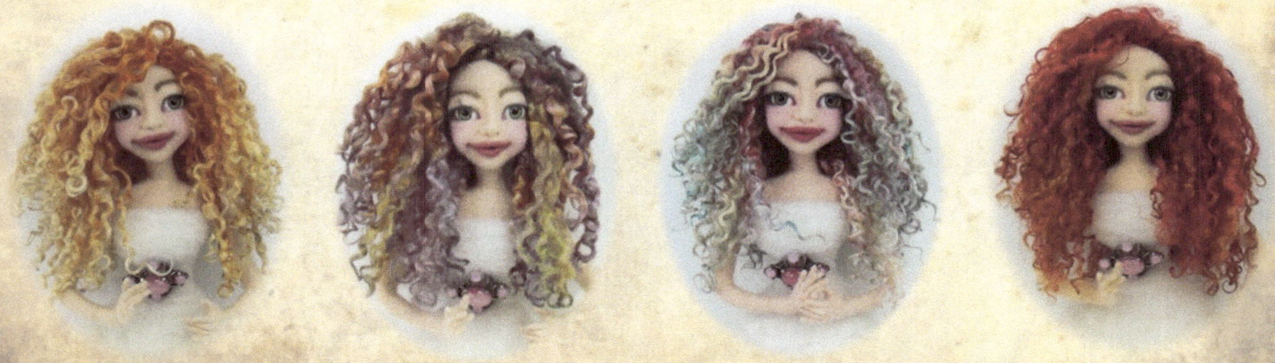

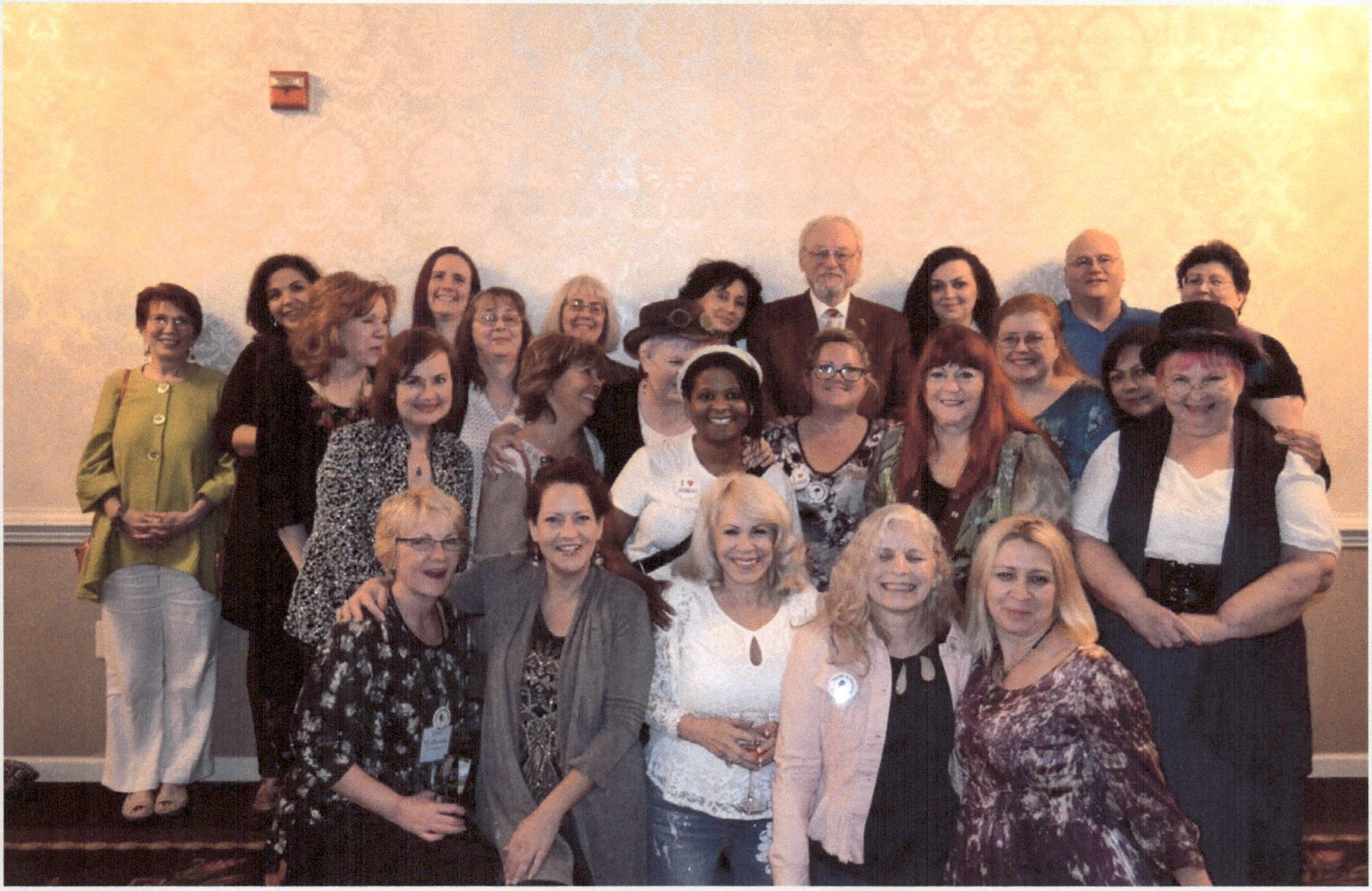

Quinlin Doll & Teddy Bear Show

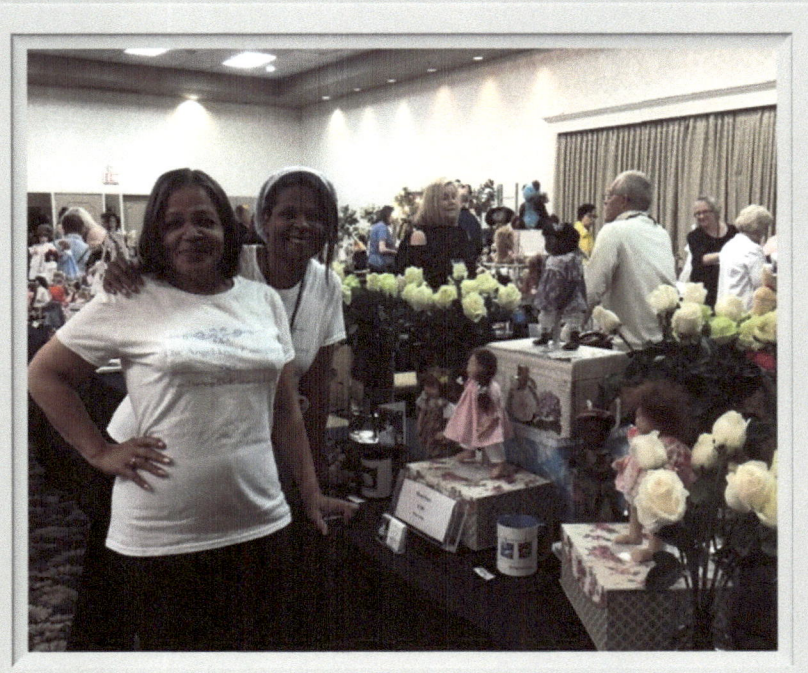

Artists from the Professional Doll Makers Art Guild attended the Quinlin Artist & Teddy Bear Convention in Philadelphia . A great pace to gather with fellow artists and friends, made our April trip a lot of fun. The show is held every year in the spring for Doll Makers and Teddy Bear Artists to market their art.

Elisabetta Visentini

Introduces "Mime"

https://www.facebook.com/elisabetta.visentini.9

elisabetta.visentini@gmail.com